P9-CQF-794

THE
POCKET
IDIOT'S
GUIDE™ TO

Bartending

by The Players and Alan Axelrod

alpha
books

A Division of Macmillan Reference USA
A Simon and Schuster Macmillan Company
1633 Broadway New York, NY 10019

For Anita—Here's looking at you, kid.

©1999 by Alan Axelrod

International Standard Book Number: 0-02-862700-8

Library of Congress Catalog Card Number: 98-88160

01 00   4 3

Interpretation of the printing code: The rightmost number of the first series of numbers is the year of the book's printing; the rightmost number of the second series of numbers is the number of the book's printing. For example, a printing code of 99-1 shows that the first printing occurred in 1999.

Printed in the United States of America

ALPHA DEVELOPMENT TEAM

Publisher
Kathy Nebenhaus

Editorial Director
Gary M. Krebs

Managing Editor
Bob Shuman

Marketing Brand Manager
Felice Primeau

Senior Editor
Nancy Mikhail

Editor
Jessica Faust

Development Editors
Maureen Horn
Phil Kitchel
Amy Zavatto

PRODUCTION TEAM

Development Editor
Maureen Horn

Production Editor
Christina Van Camp

Cover Designer
Mike Freeland

Photo Editor
Richard H. Fox

Illustrator
Jody P. Schaeffer

Designer
Kevin Spear

Indexer
Craig Small

Layout/Proofreading
Angela Calvert
Mary Hunt
Julie Trippetti

Contents

1 Garbage and Garnishes: The Basic
  Equipment of Bartending   1

2 Secrets of Measuring: Mixing and Pouring   15

3 Brother Juniper: The Joys of Gin   25

4 Na Zdorovye! The World of Vodka   39

5 The Silver Bullet   51

6 Bourbon and Whiskey   63

7 Canadian and American Whiskeys   77

8 Comin' Through the Rye   89

9 Scotch Snobs and Irish Spirits   99

10 Caribbean Sugarcane: A Rum Résumé   111

11 Tequila!   125

12 Brandies and Liqueurs   135

13 Up in Flames: Hot and Flaming Drinks   151

A Buzzed Word Glossary   165

B Last Call   173

  Index   193

Introduction

The very last person who should pick up this Pocket Idiot's Guide is an idiot. These books are for people smart enough and sensitive enough to feel like idiots about certain subjects. Most people find quantum physics an intimidating subject, but even more are snowed by mixology: the art and science of creating alcoholic—we prefer the term spiritous—drinks. What liquor to buy, what drinks to mix, how to measure them, how to mix them, how to pour them, how to serve them, and how to plan a party—these are bewilderments sufficient to reduce Albert Einstein himself to a quivering mass of Jell-O. (By the way, you will find recipes for splendid Jell-O Shots in this Pocket Guide.)

Extras

In addition to recipes, advice, guidance, and explanations, this book offers other types of information to help you mix drinks and enjoy the "pleasures of the spirit." These include definitions of key terms, tips from the world of professional bartending, a collection of popular toasts and choice barroom humor. Look for these easy-to-recognize signposts in boxes:

Buzzed Words

The vocabulary of bartending, mixology, and liquor.

Toast

Toasts—popular, unique, sincere, funny.

Quick One

Barroom humor.

Bar Tips

Expert advice on the finer points of mixology.

Trademarks

All terms mentioned in this Pocket Idiot's Guide that are known to be or are suspected of being trademarks or service marks have been appropriately capitalized. Alpha Books and Macmillan General Reference cannot attest to the accuracy of this information. Use of a term in this book should not be regarded as affecting the validity of any trademark or service mark. The following trademarks and service marks have been mentioned in this book: 7-Up, Absolut, Angostura, Appleton, Asbach-Uralt, Bacardi and Company, Bailey's Original Irish Cream, Benedictine, Bermudez, British Navy Pusser's, Cacique Ron Anejo, Captain Morgan, Chartreuse, Cherry Marnier, Coca-Cola, Cointreau, Dr. Pepper, Dubonnet, Finlandia, Glenfiddich, Glenmorangle, Grand Marnier, Hudson's Bay, Irish Mist, K.W.V., Knockando, Laphroaig, Lemon Hart & Sons, Macallan, Mandarine Napoleaon Liqueur, Metaxa, Midori, Mount Gay, Myer's Rum, Old Overholt, Pernod, Peter Heering, Peychaud's, Pisco, Presidente, Rhum Barbancourt, Ron Medellin, Rose's Lime Juice, Seagram's 7-Crown, Smirnoff, Stolichnaya, The Glenlivet, Tia Maria, Wyborowa, Zubrowka.

Chapter 1

Garbage and Garnishes: The Basic Equipment of Bartending

In This Chapter

➤ Stocking a basic liquor cabinet
➤ What you need for an advanced bar
➤ The basic and advanced mixers
➤ Glassware and other equipment

There is no "right" way to stock your bar. The liquor and the equipment you select depend on your personal needs, your taste, what you and your friends enjoy, and your budget. This chapter gives you suggestions ranging from the bare minimum to the truly well-stocked bar.

The Basics

At its most basic, the home bar can be a kitchen-cabinet collection of the two or three kinds of mixers and spirits you and your friends enjoy.

Liquors

Below are the basics for a "starter bar":

- ➤ bourbon
- ➤ Canadian whisky
- ➤ blended scotch
- ➤ gin
- ➤ light rum
- ➤ white tequila
- ➤ vodka
- ➤ brandy

Liqueurs

Even a basic bar should stock small bottles of the most popular liqueurs. Include the following:

- ➤ triple sec
- ➤ crème de menthe
- ➤ crème de cacao
- ➤ amaretto
- ➤ Kahlúa
- ➤ Drambuie
- ➤ Benedictine
- ➤ Cointreau
- ➤ Grand Marnier

Wine and Beer

For the "starter bar," stock at least the following:

- ➤ dry vermouth
- ➤ sweet vermouth
- ➤ white wine
- ➤ red wine
- ➤ champagne or sparkling wine
- ➤ beer/light beer

Mixers

You will want to stock at least five carbonated mixers:

- ➤ cola
- ➤ diet cola
- ➤ tonic water

These mix well with light alcohols, such as gin, vodka, and rum.

For the dark spirits—such as scotch and bourbon—have on hand the following:

➤ club soda

➤ ginger ale

➤ 7-Up (or the equivalent)

You'll also need five basic juices. If possible, purchase them just before use, so that they'll be fresh:

➤ orange juice

➤ grapefruit juice

➤ pineapple juice

➤ cranberry juice

➤ tomato juice

A number of drinks call for *sour mix* or *bar mix* (which is the same thing). You can buy this bottled or in ready-to-mix powdered form at liquor stores or grocery stores, or, if you prefer, you can prepare it yourself. There are two basic recipes.

Sour Mix Recipe 1

Juice of $1/2$ lemon per drink

1 tsp. sugar per drink

Simply combine these with other drink ingredients in a shaker with ice. Shake vigorously.

Commercial powdered sour mix adds powdered egg white to the product to make the drink foam up. Shaking the cocktail vigorously should provide plenty of foam, even without the egg white, but if you want to ensure a foamy sour, use the following recipe:

Sour Mix Recipe 2

12 oz. lemon juice (the juice of 6 lemons)

18 oz. distilled water

$^1/_4$ cup refined sugar

1 egg white

Blend all ingredients in a blender. Refrigerate.

Note: The mix will keep for about a week under refrigeration. You must shake or blend before each use.

Round out the "starter bar" basic mixer arsenal with:

➤ 1 small bottle of Rose's lime juice

➤ Superfine granulated sugar

➤ Coarse (not table) salt (for margaritas and Salty Dogs)

➤ Grenadine

➤ Sugar syrup (also known as simple syrup)

Bar Tips

You can buy sugar syrup ready-made or prepare it at home. In a saucepan, gradually dissolve 2 cups of sugar in a cup of water. Simmer for 10 minutes, stirring frequently. Refrigerate until needed.

One Step Beyond

If "basic" isn't enough for you, here's the next logical step. To the "starter bar," add the following spirits:

- ➤ Dutch (Genever) gin
- ➤ English gin
- ➤ Scandinavian or Russian vodka
- ➤ rye
- ➤ Irish whiskey
- ➤ single-malt scotch
- ➤ bourbon or Tennessee whiskey
- ➤ gold rum
- ➤ dark (Jamaican) rum
- ➤ gold tequila (*tequila anejo*)

There is a wide range of exotic liqueurs available. Consider the following additions to the basic roster:

- ➤ crème de cassis
- ➤ sambuca
- ➤ peppermint schnapps
- ➤ peach schnapps
- ➤ Galliano
- ➤ Frangelico

You can add any number of great wines and beers to your collection. Do consider:

- ➤ aperitif wines (Dubonnet, Lillet, and Campari are the most popular)
- ➤ cream sherry
- ➤ port
- ➤ madeira
- ➤ amontillado

Get at least two or three flavored brandies:

- ➤ Calvados or applejack (apple brandy)
- ➤ apricot brandy
- ➤ peach brandy

In addition to the most-requested mixers, you might also keep on hand the following:

➤ coffee

➤ cream (heavy and light)

➤ cream of coconut

➤ bitters

Bar Tips

Bitters is an *alcoholic* mixer (Angostura bitters is the best known) that gives a special piquance to Manhattans, old-fashioneds, and even Bloody Marys. Be careful *not* to use it to flavor non-alcoholic drinks for non-drinkers.

Garnishes and Garbage

Many mixed drinks have solid as well as liquid components. If a piece of fruit or vegetable added to a drink changes the way it tastes, then it is a *garnish*. If it's just for decoration, it's *garbage*.

The basic bar should have the following garnishes and garbage available:

Lemon twists All you use is the peel. The way to get the most peel from each lemon is to slice off the ends, then use a spoon to force the fruit out one end. Now you have an empty lemon peel. Slice it lengthwise into strips one-quarter inch wide. When a drink calls for a "twist," take one of the strips, twist it over the drink, rub the inside of the peel around the edge of the glass, plunk it in, then stir.

Lime wedges   Lime is rarely cut into twist strips; you use it in wedges.

Orange slices   Do not squeeze the orange into the drink.

Maraschino cherries   These super-sweet, surrealistically red (-dyed) little numbers are garbage; that is, they add no flavor to the drink. However, drinkers like to pull them out of the drink and eat them, so make certain you leave the stems on.

Olives   Most martini drinkers like their libation with an olive or three. Use medium-size green pitted olives—and hold the pimento (it will discolor the drink). Usually, the olive(s) are skewered on a toothpick or little plastic sword and placed in the drink.

Pearl onions   A martini harboring a pearl onion (or two or three) rather than an olive or olives is a Gibson. Stored under refrigeration in their own juice, they'll keep indefinitely. The pearls may be skewered on a toothpick.

Celery stalks   These add the finishing touch to a Bloody Mary. To add some flair, leave the stalk's leafy end on.

Buzzed Words

A **garnish** is a bit of fruit or vegetable added to a drink principally to enhance its flavor. **Garbage** is a bit of fruit or vegetable added to a drink primarily for the sake of appearance. It does not significantly enhance the flavor of the drink.

Additions

Don't forget cocktail toothpicks or, if you yearn for a touch of kitsch, little plastic cocktail swords. You'll also need swizzle sticks or cocktail straws.

Tools of the Trade

There's a load of gadgets and glassware a bartender can buy. Some of them are even useful.

| Cocktail shaker | Speedpourer | Strainer | Jigger-pony measure |

Shaker Upper

The trademark of the pro is the cocktail shaker. You'll need one to make sours, daiquiris, margaritas, and a straight-up martini à la James Bond. ("Shaken, not stirred.") Buy one with a stainless steel shell—the bigger, outer part—and glass, the smaller, inner part. A 12-ounce shaker should be ample.

You'll also need a cocktail strainer that fits over the shaker so you can pour the chilled drink without disgorging the ice cubes. This is called pouring a drink "straight-up."

Other Essentials

If you're going for that pro look, you'll also want a number of *speedpourers*—the plastic gadgets that fit into the mouth of a liquor bottle, allowing you to pour the liquor at an even, measured rate without spilling.

While you're at it, why not buy a genuine *bar spoon*? This has a small paddle spoon at one end of a long handle that is twisted in the middle. The spoon is the bartender's

Swiss army knife: Drinks can be stirred with the handle, garnishes can be manipulated with the spoon (if you don't want to use your fingers), and the swirled part can be used to pour the ingredients of layered drinks—such as pousse-cafés—in which it is important to not mix the layers.

Other equipment you are likely to already have in your kitchen:

➤ A paring knife for cutting fruit garnishes

➤ An electric blender

➤ An ice bucket with ice tongs (for the fastidious and hygienic)

A Glass Act

Glassware is far less critical in serving liquor than it is in serving fine wine. However, glass size and shape can enhance or detract from the experience of enjoying straight liquor as well as mixed drinks. Let's go over the basics.

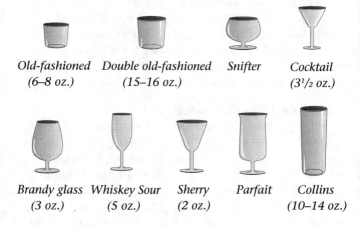

Old-fashioned   Double old-fashioned   Snifter   Cocktail
(6–8 oz.)   (15–16 oz.)   (3¹/₂ oz.)

Brandy glass   Whiskey Sour   Sherry   Parfait   Collins
(3 oz.)   (5 oz.)   (2 oz.)   (10–14 oz.)

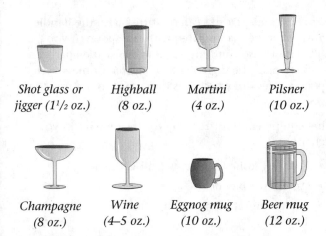

| *Shot glass or jigger (1½ oz.)* | *Highball (8 oz.)* | *Martini (4 oz.)* | *Pilsner (10 oz.)* |

| *Champagne (8 oz.)* | *Wine (4–5 oz.)* | *Eggnog mug (10 oz.)* | *Beer mug (12 oz.)* |

Highball and Low

The *highball glass* is the one you'll use most. Highball glasses are used for scotch and soda, bourbon and water, gin and tonic—you get the picture. The orthodox highball glass is a tall 8 ounces; however, some hold 12 ounces.

Only slightly less popular is the *lowball glass*, which some bartenders call a *rocks glass*, since it is used for many drinks served on the rocks. Ranging from four to nine ounces, this short, clear glass is used for martinis on the rocks, various whiskey-rocks combinations, Manhattans on the rocks, and so on.

Collins and Old-Fashioned

The *Collins glass* is not just for the Tom Collins, but for any of the larger mixed drinks that benefit from a cooling, refreshing image. This includes the various fizzes and a wealth of tropical drinks. The 10- to 14-ounce Collins glass is frosted (sometimes with an icy pebble effect as well) to about ³/₄" from the top. *Old-fashioned glasses* come in two sizes, large (7-ounce) and small (4-ounce), and are similar to the lowball glass, except for the bump at the base of the glass. Presumably, this is to remind the bartender to prepare the fixings for the old-fashioned.

Bar Tips

The Collins glass would be the same as a large (12-ounce) highball glass, except that the highball glass is entirely clear, whereas the Collins glass is partially frosted.

Cocktail and Sour

The classic *cocktail glass* is so classic—an inverted cone perched on a long stem—that it is, quite literally, *the* icon of the cocktail lounge, often immortalized in neon signs. The 4-ounce glass is used for any cocktail ordered straight-up. Its stem is more than decorative: Since drinks served in cocktail glasses have no ice in them, the stem enables you to hold the glass without warming the contents with your hands. You might add a few 4- or 5-ounce *sour glasses* to your collection. These are stemmed glasses with elongated bowls that make whiskey sours (and other foamy sour drinks) more inviting.

Wine and Sherry

The subject of wine glasses is complex. If you enjoy fine wines, read *The Complete Idiot's Guide to Wine*, which includes a discussion of glassware. For the basic bar, however, the sturdy, stemmed, globe-bowled glasses of a Parisian-style bistro are adequate.

You may also stock some *sherry glasses*. These $2^{1}/_{2}$- to $3^{1}/_{2}$-ounce stemmed glasses can be used for aperitifs and port as well as sherry. The best kind of sherry glass is the *copita*, which features a narrow taper that captures the wine's aroma. If you prefer, however, you might serve these drinks in the smaller *pony* or *cordial* glasses.

Champagne American Style and in the European Mood

Americans tend to favor a stemmed glass that looks like a shorter, wider, shallower version of the cocktail glass. It holds 4 to 6 ounces of bubbly. Europeans, however, prefer a very different glass, the champagne flute, which is tall and fluted—bulging gracefully at the bottom and tapering toward the rim.

We recommend the European flute over the American champagne glass. Not only does it hold more of a good thing (capacities vary from 7 to 11 ounces), but, more important, its tapered profile reduces the surface area and slows the dissipation of the bubbles.

Bar Tips

Using champagne flutes results in less spillage than American-style champagne glasses.

Small Stuff: The Cordial Pony and Your Best Shot

Every bar should have a supply of shot glasses, which you can use not only to serve shots, but also to measure drinks. Shot glasses come in 1- to 2-ounce sizes, and your wisest choice is 1^1/$_2$ ounces—a *jigger*—because this is the ideal size for measuring most drinks.

Buzzed Words

A **jigger** is the glass or the metal measuring cup used to measure drinks. It is also what you call the amount the jigger measures: $1^1/_2$ ounces. Strictly speaking, a **pony** is a 1-ounce measure; however, pony glasses range in capacity from 1 to 2 ounces.

Snifter Story

The *brandy snifter* is a particularly elegant piece of glassware. It ranges anywhere from about 5 to 25 ounces; however, no snifter is meant to hold so vast an amount of brandy. Opt for about a 16-ounce snifter, in which you serve no more than 1 or 2 ounces of brandy. The idea is that the oversized balloon shape will waft and funnel the aroma of the wine into the drinker's nose. If you use a snifter smaller than 16 ounces, reduce the amount of brandy proportionately.

Mugs and Pilsner Glasses

Should you choose mugs, pilsner glasses, or both? Mugs won't break as easily, but if you are serving really wonderful premium beer, the tall, elegant *pilsner glass* can enhance the drinking experience. It's your call. In either case, drinking beer from a mug or glass is far more enjoyable than sucking on a bottle or slurping from a can.

Other Specialized Glassware

Now that you've had a rundown of the basic bar glassware, you should also know about the following specialized glasses.

➤ **Pousse-café glass** A 3- to 4-ounce stemmed glass with little or no flare or tapering of the bowl. It is handy for layered dessert drinks.

➤ **Parfait glass** A slightly larger version of the pousse-café glass, the parfait glass usually has a flared lip. It is also used for layered dessert drinks.

➤ **Fizz glass** This 5-ounce stemmed glass is shorter but wider than a 5-ounce sour glass. It is useful if you want to serve fizz drinks in something smaller than a Collins glass.

➤ **Martini glass** Some people prefer their martini in this modified version of a cocktail glass rather than in a cocktail glass. Typically 4 ounces, the martini glass tapers to a very shallow point at the stem, unlike the cocktail glass, which tapers to an acute point.

➤ **Eggnog mug** This large, barrel-shaped mug is a fun way to enjoy eggnog drinks.

Do you really need any of these? Base your decisions on your taste, on what you and your guests like to drink, and on just how "complete" a host/bartender you want (and can afford) to be.

Chapter 2

Secrets of Measuring: Mixing and Pouring

In This Chapter

➤ The three basic kinds of drinks

➤ Methods of measuring

➤ When (and how) to stir, when (and how) to shake

➤ Pouring like a pro

➤ Preparing your glassware

If you've comparison-shopped before buying this book—or if you've been disloyal and mistrustful enough to consult another book after purchasing this one—you may have been overwhelmed by the sheer number of drinks it is possible to mix.

Don't panic. The fact is, almost all of those hundreds, even thousands, of "different" drinks are variations on three basic themes: the highball, the stirred cocktail ("lowball"), and the shaken cocktail. Master the themes, and you'll have no trouble with the variations. This chapter will show you how.

Bar Tips
Buy one pound of ice per each guest at a four-hour party, unless you know it's primarily a beer-and-wine crowd.

The Jigger Method

Having laid your two-thirds–ice foundation, pour in one jigger (that is, 1¹/₂ ounces) of liquor. Either use a jigger measure or a jigger-size shot glass. Then pour in the mixer—right to the top. Not only will this give you the proper liquor-to-mixer proportion for taste, it *looks* generous. Most important, it will keep you from mixing your drinks too strong. Your object is to dispense enjoyment, not intoxication.

If the mixer is carbonated, your work is done (unless the drink calls for the addition of a garnish) because the bubbles, not you, do the mixing. Indeed, resist the temptation to stir. Doing so will only accelerate the dissipation of the bubbles, and the drink will taste flat.

If the mixer is noncarbonated, either give the drink a few quick stirs with your bar spoon or just put a straw in the glass and let the drinker stir to his or her heart's content.

The Three-Count Technique

If you use a speedpourer (see the previous chapter), which provides a steady, controllable, even flow of liquor, you might want to use the Three-Count Technique. Of the three measuring techniques, it's the only one that calls for practice. Here's how to do it:

1. After filling a highball glass two-thirds with ice, grab the liquor bottle firmly by the neck. The bottle *must* have a speedpourer inserted!

2. In a single, quick motion, invert the bottle— *completely upside down*—over the glass.

3. Count to three. (Not out loud. And don't move your lips.)

The object is to practice to the point that a three count ("one-thousand one, one-thousand two, one-thousand three…") will dispense 1¹/₂ ounces. You'll probably want to practice with water in a shot glass until you've got the cadence matched with the pour rate.

Why bother?

This is a virtuoso method that makes you look like a pro. Moreover, once you've got it down, you won't have to think about counting. Your sense of timing will kick in automatically. The result will be effortless and rapid drink preparation.

Bar Tips

It pays to practice the Three-Count Technique. Once you match three counts with a 1¹/₂ ounce pour, you can match one count to one half ounce—and four counts will give you two ounces—should you ever need to deviate from the standard jigger.

Shaken, or Stirred?

So what's the big deal when Agent 007 suavely orders his martini, specifying that it be "shaken, not stirred"? It's unorthodox, that's what. It's bold and daring—as befits a secret agent who has license to kill.

For the classic martini is stirred, not shaken. Arguably, shaking rather than stirring the martini "improves" its taste by aerating the drink. Maybe. But it also may cloud the martini with tiny air bubbles—not aesthetically pleasing. Here's the accepted rule of thumb: If a drink consists of clear, relatively thin ingredients (such as the gin and vermouth of a martini), use the "least invasive" blending method—that is, stirring. If, however, a drink contains thicker fluids, such as fruit juice, shaking is required to blend the drink properly.

Toast
May you live as long as you want to, and want to as long as you live.

The Stirred Cocktail
Stirred drinks may be prepared on the rocks or straight-up. Let's walk through the mixing of a vodka gimlet as an example of a stirred cocktail prepared and served on the rocks:

1. Fill a lowball glass almost to the rim with ice.
2. Pour in 2 ounces of vodka.
3. Add 1/4 ounce of Rose's lime juice.
4. Stir *well*.
5. Garnish with a lime wedge; drop it in.

That's one way to do it. You can also prepare on-the-rocks, stirred cocktails in a two-step process. Another vodka gimlet, please:

1. Fill a shaker glass (the small, inner part of a cocktail shaker) two-thirds with ice.

2. Add 1 ounce of Rose's lime juice.

3. Pour in 5 ounces of vodka.

4. Stir vigorously. The objective is to let the ice thoroughly chill the drink.

5. Strain the gimlet into a lowball glass large enough to accommodate it—or divide the drink between two smaller lowball glasses.

6. Garnish with a lime wedge.

The process of making a drink straight-up is identical to the two-step method of preparing a drink on the rocks except that, instead of straining the chilled drink into a glass filled with ice, you just pour it into an empty, preferably chilled, glass. The key step is stirring vigorously and for a generous span of time—perhaps a count of 10 or 15. The drink really has to chill.

Great Shakes

Serious bartenders have always taken great pride in the panache with which they wield the cocktail shaker. And, despite the risk of catastrophic spillage, the secret is to be bold, vigorous, aggressive, even. Shake *hard*.

The following is the procedure for shaking a classic shaken drink, the whiskey sour:

1. Into a shaker glass two-thirds full of ice, pour 2 ounces of Canadian whisky.

2. Add 1 $^1/_2$ ounces of sour mix.

3. Take the stainless steel shell of the cocktail shaker and put it on top of the glass. Press down *firmly* in order to create a leak-proof seal. The beauty of the steel shell is that it will contract during shaking, because the icy fluid lowers its temperature.

4. Use both hands. Put one hand on top of the shaker, and the other on the bottom. Grasp firmly. Shake hard for at least six counts.

5. If you've done everything right, the laws of physics will have created a stout seal between the stainless steel top and the glass bottom of the shaker. To break the seal, so that you can get at the drink, look for the frost line on the steel shell. That's where the top and bottom are sealed. Firmly tap this line with the heel of your hand. You should hear a snap—that's the seal breaking.

6. The shell will now come off very easily. *But don't take it off yet.* First turn the shaker over, so that the steel shell is on the bottom. This will prevent spillage. *Now* take the glass out.

7. Strain the drink from the steel shell into a lowball glass or into a whiskey-sour glass, if you have one. The advantage of the whiskey-sour glass is that, if the drinker handles it by the stem, the straight-up drink will stay colder longer.

8. Garnish. The classic finishing touches are a maraschino cherry inside the glass and an orange or lemon slice perched on the lip of the glass.

There is a downside to shaken drinks: the clean-up. Unless you are making one right after the other of the same drink, you'll need to clean the shaker immediately. It will get gummy and nasty if you don't. Rinse it with water, then wipe it out.

Quick One

There was a college that had the reputation of being a fountain of knowledge. Everyone went there to drink.

Mix, Blend, and Puree!

Given a shaker and sufficient elbow grease on the part of the bartender, shaking is sufficient to blend most drinks. However, if you want to prepare frozen drinks, such as a frozen margarita, a frozen daiquiri, or a frozen piña colada, you'll need an electric blender.

First, make sure that your blender is up to the task of handling ice. A heavy-duty model is best. Then:

1. Make sure the motor is off. Pour the liquor into the blender. Next come the mixers, then the fruit. Last: Add ice—enough to fill the blender to three-quarters full.

2. Make sure you put the lid on properly. Hold it down with one hand and start the machine at low speed. Once the initial mixing is complete, switch to high until everything is thoroughly blended.

3. Pour the drink directly into glasses. No straining is necessary because the ice has been crushed and blended with the drink.

Buzzed Words

Frozen drinks are also called **freezes**.

Popping Your Cork

To open wine, begin by completely removing the foil "capsule" from the top of the bottle. If you are using the popular waiter's corkscrew, insert the point of the helical screw (called a "worm") into the cork slightly off center. Bore deeply into the cork, then pull straight up, twisting slightly to loosen the cork. An easier alternative is to use

either a twin-lever corkscrew or a screwpull-type corkscrew. These are available in most stores that sell food-
preparation utensils.

Opening champagne is at once easier and more challenging than opening a bottle of wine. It's easier, because you
don't have to use a corkscrew. It's more challenging because the contents of the bottle are under great pressure.

➤ Inspect the bottle before opening it. Look for deep
scratches or nicks. Deep imperfections in the glass
may cause the bottle to explode.

➤ Do not chill champagne below 45 degrees. Chilling
below this temperature increases the potential for an
explosion.

➤ During the uncorking process, point the bottle away
from you and others.

To remove the cork, point the bottle away from you and
others, and remove the foil "capsule" covering the top.
Next, untwist the wire cage that is over the cork. While
doing this, place your palm over the cork to keep it from
shooting out of the bottle. Now, still pointing the bottle
away from all living beings, gently twist the cork, cupping
your palm over it. As the cork works free, it will press
against your palm. Do not release the cork. Do not let it
pop. It should clear the bottle with a barely audible hiss or
very muffled pop.

Using the Speedpourer

We've already discussed the speedpourer as absolutely required for bartenders using the Three-Count Method.
Even if you don't use that method, however, speedpourers
make your job quicker and neater. Do take time to put the
speedpourer in the bottle so that the slant of the mouth is
at a right angle to the label. This will put more speed into
your pour by allowing you to grab the bottle without having to check which way the stream of liquor will emerge.

Moreover, your guests will be able to see the label as your pour—a nice touch, especially if you are serving premium liquor.

Developing a Multiple Personality

If you've admired the speed of the super-fast bartender who can prepare multiples of the same drink simultaneously, now is your chance to admire yourself. *You* can do it!

Just line up X number of glasses in a row. They should be filled with ice, and they should be standing rim to rim. Make sure a speedpourer is in the bottle of booze. Grab the bottle by the neck. Do a smooth inversion over the first glass, count three, move the still-inverted bottle smoothly to the next glass, count three, go on and on and on.

Unfortunately, because you can't put a speedpourer into most mixer bottles, you'll have to pour this ingredient in one glass at a time. Same goes for dispensing the garnish.

Toast

Here's to wives and sweethearts—may they never meet!

Chilling

If you want to chill a glass before pouring a drink into it, refrigerate the dry glass for an hour or longer, then fill the glass with ice water. Prepare the drink. When you are ready to pour the drink, dump out the ice water.

Frosting

Frosting is a step beyond chilling. Dip the glass in water, then put it in the freezer for half an hour. This will give it a frosty white appearance. If the glass has a stem, hold it by the stem to avoid melting any of the frost.

Salting

Salting means rimming the glass with salt—something you may want to do for a Salty Dog or a margarita. It's easy if you remember to use rock salt rather than table salt.

Pour rock salt on a plate. Take a lime wedge and rub it around the rim of glass. Roll the glass rim around in the salt.

Flavoring the Rim

Aside from salting, you can flavor the rim of any glass with the fruit used to garnish the drink. Just run the orange, lime, or lemon peel on the rim. It will impart a subtle flavor and aroma to the drink.

Bar Tips

Tips on preparing lemon twists, lime wedges, orange slices, and other garnishes and "garbage" are found in Chapter 1.

Chapter 3

Brother Juniper: The Joys of Gin

In This Chapter

➤ How gin is made
➤ The range of flavorfulness of gin
➤ Gin recipes

A deeply aromatic spirit, gin doesn't appeal to everybody, but those who admire it cherish its bracing, refreshing qualities, redolent of juniper berries and a host of other *botanicals*—an often exotic collection of extracts from roots, barks, seeds, and leaves—that give gin its character. Unlike vodka, which is (or should be) flavorless, the character of gin varies greatly from brand to brand and invites a lot of "comparison shopping."

Buzzed Words

Gins are often designated **dry gin** or **London dry gin**. These originated when "sweet" (called **Old Tom**) as well as "dry" gin was available. Today, the distinction is mainly superfluous, because almost all English and American gin is now dry. Also note that London dry gin doesn't have to be made in London or even England. This describes a manufacturing style, not a place of origin.

Gin and...

Although not everyone likes the taste of gin by itself, it vies with vodka as the most mixable of spirits. It can be combined with just about anything.

Bar Tips

An open bottle of tonic water or club soda is only good for about a day. To make sure they're always crisp, consider buying them in six packs of small bottles, which you can finish before they get flat. For a big party, go for the larger bottles.

Gin and Bitters

Serve straight-up, strained into an old-fashioned or lowball glass.

2 oz. gin

$^1/_2$ tsp. Angostura bitters

Stir the gin and bitters in a glass with ice cubes until well chilled. Strain into the serving glass.

Gin and Campari

Serve in a lowball glass.

$1^1/_2$ oz. gin

$1^1/_2$ oz. Campari

Orange slice or twist of orange

Combine gin and Campari in a cocktail shaker with ice. Shake vigorously, then strain into the serving glass filled with ice. Garnish with an orange slice or a twist of orange.

Gin and Sin

Serve straight-up, strained into a cocktail glass.

2 oz. gin

1 tbs. Cinzano

Combine gin and Cinzano in a glass with ice, stir until well chilled, then strain into the serving glass.

Gin and Ginger

Serve on the rocks in a chilled highball glass.

$1^1/_2$ oz. gin

Ginger ale to fill

Lemon twist

Combine gin and ginger ale in the serving glass filled with ice. Drop in the lemon twist.

Negroni

Serve straight-up in a chilled cocktail glass.

2 oz. gin

$^1/_2$ oz. sweet vermouth

$^3/_4$ oz. Campari

Splash of club soda (optional)

Orange peel

Combine all ingredients, except the orange peel, in a shaker with ice. Shake vigorously, then strain into the serving glass. Twist the orange peel and drop into the glass.

Gin and Soda

Serve on the rocks in a highball glass.

$1^1/_2$–2 oz. gin

Club soda to fill

Lemon twist

Pour the gin into the serving glass filled with ice. Add club soda, and garnish with the lemon twist.

Gin and Tonic
Serve on the rocks in a highball glass.

2–2¹/₂ oz. gin

Tonic water to fill

Lime wedge or lemon twist

Pour the gin into the serving glass filled with ice. Add tonic, and garnish with a lime wedge (traditional) or, if you prefer, a lemon twist.

Bar Tips

Don't look for a martini here. It gets its own chapter: Chapter 5, "The Silver Bullet."

Gimlet Eye

Gimlet with Fresh Lime
Serve in a chilled old-fashioned or lowball glass.

2 oz. gin

¹/₂ oz. fresh lime (or limon) juice

Lime twist or lime slice

Stir gin and juice very vigorously in a mixing (shaker) glass with cracked ice; pour into the serving glass. Garnish with a lime twist or lime slice. May also be served straight-up: Stir with ice cubes, then strain into the serving glass.

Gimlet with Rose's Lime Juice
Serve in a chilled old-fashioned or lowball glass.

2 oz. gin

$^1/_2$ oz. Rose's lime juice

Lime slice

Use a shaker or blender to mix the gin and Rose's with cracked ice; pour into the serving glass. The best garnish is a lime slice, which gets more of the natural juice into the drink. May also be served straight-up: Strain the shaken or blended ingredients into the serving glass.

Tom Collins
Serve on the rocks in a Collins or highball glass.

2–3 oz. gin

$1^1/_2$ oz. lemon juice

$1^1/_2$ oz. sugar syrup

Club soda to fill

Maraschino cherry

Combine all ingredients except club soda and cherry in the serving glass with ice. Stir well. Fill with club soda, and garnish with the cherry.

Juices (Mostly)

Most of us are familiar with vodka and orange juice (the screwdriver) and with vodka and grapefruit juice. No law says you can't substitute gin for vodka in these faithful standbys.

Gin Screwdriver

Serve on the rocks in a highball glass.

1^1/$_2$ oz. gin

2–3 oz. orange juice

Stir well. If you like, add a dash or two of Angostura bitters.

Orange Blossom

Serve in a chilled cocktail glass.

1^1/$_2$ oz. gin

1 oz. orange juice

Orange slice

Combine all ingredients, except the orange slice, in a shaker with ice. Shake vigorously, then strain into the serving glass. Garnish with the orange slice.

Abbey

Serve on the rocks in a lowball glass.

1^1/$_2$ oz. gin

1^1/$_2$ oz. orange juice

Dash or 2 of orange bitters

Maraschino cherry

Combine all ingredients, except for the cherry, in a shaker with ice. Shake vigorously, then strain into the ice-filled serving glass. Garnish with the cherry.

Bronx Cocktail

Serve straight-up in a chilled cocktail glass.

1½ oz. gin

½ oz. orange juice

Dash of dry vermouth

Dash of sweet vermouth

Combine all ingredients, with ice, in a shaker. Shake vigorously. Strain into the serving glass. Some drinkers prefer more of the vermouths—½ ounce each—and a full ounce of orange juice. If you want a dry cocktail, skip the sweet vermouth.

Lone Tree

Serve straight-up in a chilled cocktail glass.

¾ oz. gin

¾ oz. dry vermouth (optional)

¼ oz. sweet vermouth

Several dashes of orange bitters (optional)

Olive (optional)

To a shaker filled with cracked ice add all ingredients except for the olive. Shake vigorously. Strain into the serving glass and garnish with the olive.

Abbey Cocktail

Serve straight-up in a chilled cocktail glass.

1¹/₂ oz. gin

¹/₄ oz. orange juice

³/₄ oz. sweet vermouth

Dash or 2 of Angostura bitters

Maraschino cherry

Combine all ingredients, except for the cherry, in a shaker with ice. Shake vigorously, then strain into the serving glass. Garnish with the cherry.

Gin Sour

Serve straight-up in a whiskey sour glass or lowball glass.

2–3 oz. gin

1 oz. lemon juice

1 tsp. sugar syrup

Orange or lemon slice

Maraschino cherry

In a shaker, with ice, combine all ingredients except the garnishes. Shake vigorously. Strain into the serving glass. Garnish with an orange slice and maraschino cherry.

A Fizz and a Rickey

Buzzed Words
A **rickey** is any drink with soda water and lime—and sometimes sugar.

Gin Fizz

Serve on the rocks in a Collins or tall highball glass.

1¹/₂ oz. gin

1 tbs. powdered sugar

3 oz. sour mix

Club soda to fill

Maraschino cherry

Orange slice

To a shaker filled with ice add the gin, sugar, and sour mix. Shake vigorously. Pour into the ice-filled serving glass, then add club soda. Garnish with a maraschino cherry and an orange slice.

Gin Daisy
Serve in a chilled highball glass.

2–3 oz. gin

1 oz. lemon juice

$^1/_4$ oz. raspberry syrup or grenadine

$^1/_2$ tsp. sugar syrup

Club soda to fill

Orange slice

To a shaker filled with cracked ice add all ingredients except for the club soda and orange slice. Shake vigorously. Pour into the serving glass. Add club soda to fill, then garnish with the orange slice.

Gin Rickey
Serve on the rocks in a highball glass.

$1^1/_2$ oz. gin

Club soda to fill

Juice of $^1/_2$ fresh lime

Fill a highball glass half full of ice cubes; pour in the gin, then the club soda to fill. Add the lime juice.

Gin Sidecar
Serve in a chilled old-fashioned or lowball glass.

$1^1/_2$ oz. gin

$^3/_4$ oz. triple sec

1 oz. lemon juice

Pour all ingredients into a shaker with cracked ice. Shake vigorously. Pour into the serving glass.

Liqueur Refreshed, Brandy Rebranded— and a Dash of Dubonnet

Liqueur: heavy, sweet, and ideal for dessert drinks. That's a true assessment as far as it goes, but, if you know how to combine gin and liqueur, you'll see that this truism just doesn't go far enough. Neither liqueur nor flavored brandy need be reserved just for desserts.

Slings are sweet drinks made with brandy, whiskey, or gin. Here's the gin version.

Cornell Cocktail
Serve straight-up in a chilled cocktail glass.

4 oz. gin

1 oz. Maraschino liqueur

1 egg white *

Vigorously shake all ingredients with ice in a shaker or blend; strain into the serving glasses. *Recipe makes two drinks.*

* Raw egg may be a source of salmonella bacteria. You may wish to avoid drinks calling for raw egg yolk or white.

Gin Sling
Serve in an old-fashioned or lowball glass.

2–3 oz. gin

1 oz. lemon juice

$^1/_2$ oz. orgeat or sugar syrup

Club soda to fill

Fill serving glass half full with cracked ice. Add all ingredients except club soda. Stir. Add club soda to fill. If you don't want a fizzy drink, substitute plain water for the club soda.

Buzzed Words

A **sling** is any brandy, whiskey, or gin drink that is sweetened and flavored with lemon.

Tropical Heritage

Bermuda Cocktail

Serve in a chilled old-fashioned or lowball glass.

1¹/₂ oz. gin

1 oz. apricot brandy

¹/₂ oz. lime juice (fresh or Rose's)

1 tsp. Falernum or sugar syrup

Dash of grenadine

Orange peel

¹/₂ tsp. curaçao

To a shaker filled with cracked ice add all ingredients except the orange peel and curaçao. Shake vigorously. Pour into the serving glass. Garnish with the orange peel twist, then carefully top with curaçao so that it floats.

Singapore Sling

Serve on the rocks in a chilled Collins or highball glass.

2 oz. gin

1 oz. cherry brandy or
Peter Heering

Juice of 1/2 lemon

Dash of Benedictine

Club soda to fill

Lemon slice

Mint sprig

In a shaker with cracked ice combine all ingredients
except for the lemon slice and mint sprig, but
including a splash of club soda. Shake vigorously.
Strain into the serving glass. Add ice cubes and club
soda to fill. Garnish with lemon slice and mint sprig.

Pink Lady

Serve straight-up in a chilled cocktail glass.

3 oz. gin

3 oz. applejack or Calvados

2 oz. lemon juice

2 tsp. sugar syrup

2 tsp. grenadine

1 egg white *

Combine all ingredients, with ice, in a shaker. Shake
vigorously. Strain into serving glasses. Recipe makes
two drinks.

* *Raw egg may be a source of salmonella bacteria. You
may wish to avoid drinks calling for raw egg yolk or white.*

Gin and Grapefruit Juice

Serve on the rocks in a highball glass.

1 1/2 oz. gin

2–3 oz. grapefruit juice

Combine all ingredients in a serving glass filled
with ice. Stir well.

Chapter 4

Na Zdorovye!
The World of Vodka

In This Chapter

➤ Vodka comes to America

➤ The art of flavoring vodka

➤ The Bloody Mary—history and recipes

➤ Favorite vodka recipes

Colorless, tasteless, and aromaless, vodka outsells any other category of spirits in the United States. This may strike you as surprising when you consider that vodka was rarely consumed here before World War II.

It would make for exciting reading if we could tell you that American soldiers brought the stuff home from war-torn Russia, but that's not the case. World War II saw the American people subjected to rigorous rationing of almost every product they had previously taken for granted. Alcoholic beverages were no exception. With peace came an end to rationing, but, after four years of war, liquor dealers had precious little product to offer.

Straight, No Chaser

By U.S. law, all non-flavored vodka consumed here must be filtered after distillation to remove all distinctive character, aroma, taste, and color. However, even the flavorless vodkas—especially the premium brands—do have a certain character, an undertone of flavor, which partisans of particular brands prize.

Bloody Mary

Now, some folks just throw a little vodka and a little tomato juice together and hand you what they call a Bloody Mary. But that's, at best, a vodka and tomato juice, not a Bloody Mary. The classic recipe, evolved and elaborated upon from Harry's original, follows.

Bloody Mary
Serve in a chilled Collins glass.

2 oz. vodka

4–6 oz. tomato juice

1 tsp. lemon juice

$1/4$ tsp. Worcestershire sauce

Few dashes Tabasco sauce

Pinch white pepper

Pinch or two of celery salt

$1/2$ tsp. dried or fresh chopped dill

Celery stalk

Combine all ingredients (except for the celery stalk) with cracked ice in a shaker. Shake gently. Pour into the serving glass. Garnish with the celery stalk and, if you wish, add two or three ice cubes.

Bar Tips
Most shaker drinks should be shaken vigorously, but not the Bloody Mary. Shake *too* hard, and the tomato juice may separate. Go gently.

Bloody Blossom
Serve in a Collins glass.

1¹/₂ oz. vodka	3 oz. tomato juice
3 oz. orange juice	Mint sprig

In a shaker, combine all ingredients except the mint sprig with cracked ice. Shake gently. Pour into the serving glass, and garnish with the mint.

Citrus Productions

Vodka mixes beautifully with citrus juices. Don't invest in premium-label vodka for citrus drinks; instead, spend a little extra to buy freshly-squeezed juices or spend a little extra time to squeeze the juice fresh yourself. You'll taste the difference.

Cape Codder
Serve in a large (double) chilled old-fashioned glass.

1¹/₂ oz. vodka	4 oz. cranberry juice
Dash lime juice	1 tsp. sugar syrup

Combine all ingredients in a shaker with cracked ice. Shake vigorously, and pour into the serving glass.

Vodka Gimlet with Fresh Lime
Serve on the rocks in a lowball glass.

2 oz. vodka

1 oz. fresh lime juice

Combine all ingredients in a shaker. Shake vigorously. Pour into the serving glass. *Or,* combine both ingredients in the serving glass and stir.

Vodka Gimlet with Rose's Lime Juice
Serve in a chilled cocktail glass.

2 oz. vodka

$1/2$ oz. Rose's lime juice

Combine both ingredients with ice in a mixing glass. Stir. Strain into the serving glass.

Screwdrivers, Wallbangers, and Other Mostly Orange Juice Drinks

To think of vodka and orange juice is to think of a screwdriver, a very basic drink named for a very basic tool. It's best if the orange juice is freshly squeezed!

Screwdriver
Serve on the rocks in a chilled highball glass or in a large (double) chilled old-fashioned glass.

$1^1/2$ oz. vodka

4 oz. orange juice

Orange slice

Fill serving glass one-third with ice cubes. Pour in vodka and orange juice, stir, and garnish with the orange slice.

Harvey Wallbanger

Serve on the rocks in a chilled Collins glass.

1^1/$_2$ oz. vodka

4 oz. orange juice

^{1}/$_2$ oz. Galliano

Fill serving glass one-third with ice cubes. Pour in vodka and orange juice, and stir. Carefully add the Galliano so that it floats. Do not stir!

Fuzzy Navel

Serve on the rocks in a highball glass.

^{3}/$_4$ oz. peach schnapps

^{3}/$_4$ oz. vodka

Orange juice to fill

Combine all ingredients in the serving glass and stir.

Original Sex on the Beach

Serve in a chilled highball glass.

1 oz. vodka

^{1}/$_2$ oz. Midori melon liqueur

^{1}/$_2$ oz. Chambord (substitute other raspberry liqueur if necessary)

1^1/$_2$ oz. pineapple juice

1^1/$_2$ oz. cranberry juice cocktail

Combine all ingredients in a shaker with ice. Shake vigorously and pour into the serving glass.

Buzzed Words

A **shooter** is a drink meant to be downed in a single shot, often accompanied by table banging and gasps of pleasurable pain.

Alternative Sex on the Beach
Serve on the rocks in a highball glass.

3/4 oz. peach schnapps

3/4 oz. vodka

3 oz. pineapple or grapefruit juice

3 oz. cranberry juice cocktail

Combine all ingredients in the serving glass with ice and stir.

Another popular shooter is the Kamikaze. Banzai!

Kamikaze
Serve in a shot glass.

1 oz. vodka

1 oz. triple sec

1 oz. lime juice

Shake with ice; strain into *three* shot glasses.

Coffee Combo

Here's a coffee and vodka drink you'll enjoy.

Black Russian
Serve in a chilled old-fashioned glass.

$1^1/_2$ oz. vodka

$^3/_4$ oz. Kahlúa

Combine the two ingredients with cracked ice in a shaker. Shake vigorously, then pour into the serving glass. Optionally, add a few dashes of lemon juice for a "Black Magic." Garnish with a lemon twist, if desired.

White Russian
Serve in a chilled cocktail glass.

$1^1/_2$ oz. vodka

1 oz. white crème de cacao

$^3/_4$ oz. heavy cream

Combine the ingredients with cracked ice in a shaker. Shake vigorously, then strain into the serving glass.

Russian Coffee
Serve in a chilled brandy snifter.

$^1/_2$ oz. vodka

$1^1/_2$ oz. coffee liqueur

1 oz. heavy cream

Combine all ingredients in a blender with ice. Blend until smooth, then pour into the snifter.

Bar Tips

Vodka is becoming increasingly popular as an alternative to gin in martinis, but don't look for your vodka martini here. You'll find it, with its gin-based brethren, in Chapter 5.

The Vodka...

Vodka Collins

Serve on the rocks in a Collins glass.

1 oz. vodka

2 oz. sour mix

Club soda to fill

Maraschino cherry

Combine all ingredients except for the cherry in the serving glass filled with ice. Stir. Garnish with the maraschino cherry.

Bar Tips

If you don't want to use store-bought sour mix, see Chapter 1 for a fresh recipe.

Vodka Cooler (Simple)
Serve on the rocks in a Collins glass.

1 oz. vodka

$^1/_2$ oz. sweet vermouth

7-Up to fill

Combine the vodka and sweet vermouth in a shaker with ice. Shake vigorously. Strain into serving glass filled with ice. Add 7-Up to fill.

Vodka Grasshopper
Serve in a chilled cocktail glass.

$^1/_2$ oz. vodka

$^3/_4$ oz. green crème de menthe

$^3/_4$ oz. white crème de menthe

Combine the ingredients with cracked ice in a shaker. Shake vigorously, then strain into the serving glass.

Flying Grasshopper
Serve in a chilled old-fashioned or lowball glass.

$1^1/_2$ oz. vodka

$^1/_2$ oz. green crème de menthe

$^1/_2$ oz. white crème de menthe

Combine all the ingredients with cracked ice in a shaker. Shake vigorously, then pour into the serving glass.

Vodka Sour
Serve straight-up in a chilled sour glass.

1^1/$_2$–2 oz. vodka	Lemon slice
^{3}/$_4$ oz. lemon juice	Maraschino cherry
1 tsp. sugar syrup	

Combine all ingredients except the lemon slice and cherry in a shaker with cracked ice. Shake vigorously. Strain into the serving glass and garnish with the lemon slice and maraschino cherry.

Vodka Stinger
Serve in a chilled cocktail glass.

1^1/$_2$ oz. vodka

1 oz. white crème de menthe

Combine all ingredients in a shaker with cracked ice. Shake vigorously and strain into the serving glass.

Vodka Tonic
Serve on the rocks in a highball glass.

1^1/$_2$ oz. vodka

Tonic water to fill

Lime wedge

Pour the vodka into a serving glass one-third full of ice. Add tonic to fill, and garnish with the lime wedge.

Melon Ball

Serve in a cocktail glass.

$^3/_4$ oz. vodka

$^1/_2$ oz. melon liqueur

2 oz. orange juice

Mix ingredients in a shaker with ice. Pour into a cocktail glass. Garnish with an orange slice.

Be inventive. The range of possible vodka combinations is limited only by your imagination. Vodka is a neutral spirit you can mix with almost anything. If you need a little help, see Appendix B for more ways to quench your thirst.

Chapter 5

The Silver Bullet

In This Chapter

➤ Martini controversies

➤ How dry is a dry martini?

➤ The basic martini

➤ Variations on the martini

The classic "three-martini lunch" has diminished in popularity since the IRS reduced the allowable deduction on business entertaining—and employers realized that *three* martinis at lunch do have a certain impact on the workday. But the martini nevertheless remains at once the most sophisticated, variable, refined, controversial, and popular of cocktails. Self-proclaimed purists have a lot to say about how a martini should be made, and that includes forbidding vodka as an ingredient. "You can make a very nice drink with vodka and vermouth," they say, "but it's not a martini."

Well, this chapter will aim to please the purists, but it will also cover the vodka as well as the gin martini—and a good many variations on these. We trust we will give no lasting offense, but purists may wish to shield their eyes.

Buzzed Words

A **dry martini** is one with relatively little vermouth versus gin. Some drinkers prefer 12 parts gin to 1 part vermouth, while others insist on a 20-to-1 ratio. Extremists do away with the vermouth altogether and have a gin and olive on the rocks.

Martini Secrets

Here are the 10 secrets of making a great martini:

1. For a gin martini, use a premium-label gin. Which one you use is up to you. They range in degree of flavorfulness. If you like a martini redolent of aromatic botanicals, veer toward the Bombay end of the gin spectrum. If you prefer a cleaner taste, lean toward Beefeater. Something in between? Taste Tanqueray. Try them all in your favorite club, then bring home your favorite.

2. For a vodka martini, use a premium-label vodka. The variations in flavorfulness and character among these are less pronounced than among premium-label gins, but you may want to sample several to find a favorite.

3. Use a dry vermouth that you would enjoy drinking by itself, on the rocks. Two brands, Noilly-Prat and Martini and Rossi, dominate the market. Both are excellent. Sample and decide.

4. Use super-clean glassware for mixing as well as for serving. Make certain there is no detergent or soap aftertaste.

5. Whether you serve your martini straight-up or on the rocks, use ice that is entirely free from freezer burn or freezer-borne smells and tastes. Commercial bagged ice is always best.

6. Never use olives stuffed with pimento. They will discolor the drink and give it an unwanted flavor.

7. But... never say never. Some martini lovers like pimento in their olive and don't mind the drink's pinkish hue and peppery flavor one bit.

8. If you are the host, *listen* to the drinker. Based on your taste and experience, you may suggest this or that ratio and this or that gin, but don't force anything on anyone. Accommodate the drinker.

9. Don't let *anyone* tell you there's only one "right" way to make a martini.

10. But it's not worth fighting over. Give peace a chance.

Quick One

An Air Force pilot always packed gin and vermouth, olives, a mixing spoon, and a chrome-plated cup. One day, his copilot asked, "What good will all that do if we crash in the jungle?" The pilot answered, "We go down in the middle of nowhere, I start making a martini, and somebody will show up and say, '*That's no way to make a martini!*'"

The Classic Dry Martini

We believe that the "dry" martini is the closest thing there is to a "standard" martini. Here's how it's done.

Dry Martini

Serve in a chilled cocktail glass.

2 oz. gin

$^1/_2$ tsp. dry vermouth

Olive or lemon twist

Combine the gin and vermouth in a mixing glass at least half full of ice. Stir well, then strain into the cocktail glass. Garnish with the olive or the lemon twist. If your olives are very small, spear three on a toothpick.

Quick One

"Let me slip out of these wet clothes and into a dry martini."

—Robert Benchley, Algonquin wit

If you want to taste more of the vermouth, make the martini less dry by adding more vermouth. Many drinkers favor a 5-to-1 ratio.

A dry vodka martini should be drier than the dry gin martini. Here's a starting point most drinkers will enjoy.

Dry Vodka Martini

Serve in a chilled cocktail glass.

3 oz. vodka

Dash of dry vermouth

Olive or lemon twist

Combine the vodka and vermouth in a mixing glass at least half full of ice. Stir well, then *quickly* strain into the cocktail glass. Garnish with the olive or the lemon twist. If your olives are very small, spear three on a toothpick.

Bar Tips

Both the gin and vodka martinis—but especially the vodka martini—benefit from quick stirring with a lot of ice rather than prolonged stirring with a few ice cubes. The object is to minimize meltage, which dilutes the drink. One of the few things martini drinkers agree on is that a watery drink stinks.

But wait—there's the *perfect* martini, then there's the *Perfect* Martini. The presumptuous name comes from the exquisite yin and yang of the sweet versus the dry vermouth.

Perfect Martini

Serve in a chilled cocktail glass.

1$\frac{1}{2}$ oz. gin

$\frac{1}{2}$ tsp. dry vermouth

$\frac{1}{2}$ tsp. sweet vermouth

Olive

Combine all ingredients except the olive in a mixing glass with ice. Stir well and strain into the serving glass. Garnish with the olive.

The Really Dry Martini

There are at least three ways to make a *really* dry martini:

1. Using the same amount of gin or vodka as for the basic dry martini, add just two or three *drops* of vermouth. No, you don't need an eye dropper. Just put your thumb over the mouth of the bottle and sprinkle.

2. Pour an ounce or so of dry vermouth into a chilled cocktail glass. Swirl the vermouth to coat the glass. Pour out the excess vermouth. Stir the gin or vodka in a mixing glass with ice. Strain into the coated cocktail glass.

3. Forget the vermouth altogether. Serve straight gin or vodka on the rocks or straight-up (having stirred the spirit with ice). Call it a *really* dry martini (but it's really just cold gin).

Gibson

The Gibson is the most common variation on the martini theme. At its most basic, it's just a martini with a few (three or more, depending on size and preference) pickled pearl onions instead of the olive or lemon twist. The conscientious Gibson maker, however, varies the underlying martini recipe slightly, yielding a somewhat larger drink that is *always* on the very dry side.

The Vodka Gibson is almost identical to the Gin Gibson. Just add a bit more vodka.

Gibson
Serve in a chilled cocktail glass.

$2^1/_2$ oz. gin

Dash or two of dry vermouth

Pickled pearl onions

Combine the gin and vermouth in a mixing glass at least half full of ice. Stir well, then *quickly* strain into the cocktail glass. Garnish with the pearl onions.

Bar Tips
Take a moment to blot the pickled pearl onions with a paper towel. This will remove excess vinegar, which might otherwise give an unwanted flavor to the drink.

Vodka Gibson
Serve in a chilled cocktail glass.

3 oz. vodka

Dash or two of dry vermouth

Pickled pearl onions

Combine the vodka and vermouth in a mixing glass at least half full of ice. Stir well, then *quickly* strain into the cocktail glass. Garnish with the pearl onions.

Bar Tips

To chill a glass, fill it with ice, add water, and let it sit while you mix the drink. When ready to pour, dump the water and ice, shake the glass to remove the excess, and pour the drink!

Vodka Varieties

Cajun Martini

Serve in a chilled cocktail glass.

3 oz. vodka

Dash dry vermouth

Thin slice of garlic

Several slices of pickled jalapeño peppers

Pickled pearl onions

At least one hour before serving, prepare the vodka by steeping the garlic, jalapeño, and onions in it. The steeping vodka should be stored in a closed container in the freezer. Combine the steeped vodka and vermouth in a mixing glass at least half full of ice. Stir well, then *quickly* strain into the cocktail glass. Garnish with a jalapeño slice or some pearl onions.

Bar Tips

Glasses stored for a long time in a closed cabinet sometimes acquire a musty, dusty taste. Rinse out even clean glasses if they have been stored for any length of time.

Spanish Vodka Martini
Serve in a chilled cocktail glass.

2$^1/_2$ oz. vodka

$^1/_2$ oz. dry sherry

Lemon twist

Combine the vodka and vermouth in a mixing glass at least half full of ice. Stir well, then *quickly* strain into the cocktail glass. Garnish with the lemon twist.

Exotic Variations

By now we've either reeducated (fat chance!) or thoroughly alienated the martini purists out there, so let's plunge ahead boldly into the depths of decadence with a catalogue of martini exotica.

Chocolate Martini
Serve in a martini glass.

2 oz. vodka

$^1/_2$ oz. creme de cacao

Combine both ingredients in a shaker filled with ice. Pour into the serving glass.

Hawaiian Martini
Serve in a chilled cocktail glass.

1$^1/_2$ oz. gin

1 tsp. dry vermouth

1 tsp. sweet vermouth

1 tsp. pineapple juice

Combine all the ingredients in a shaker with ice. Shake well, and strain into the serving glass.

Martini Romana

Serve in a chilled cocktail glass.

1^1/$_2$ oz. gin

^{1}/$_2$ tsp. dry vermouth

Few dashes of Campari

Combine all ingredients in a mixing glass with ice. Stir well and strain into the serving glass.

Rum Martini

Serve in a chilled cocktail glass.

2 oz. white rum   Olive

Several drops of dry vermouth   Lime twist

Combine the ingredients except the olive and lime twist in a mixing glass with ice. Stir well and strain into the serving glass. Garnish with the olive and lime twist.

The Tequini doffs a sombrero to the country south of the border. It's a martini made with tequila instead of gin.

Tequini

Serve in a chilled cocktail glass.

2^1/$_2$ oz. tequila

^{1}/$_2$ oz. dry vermouth

Olive or lemon twist

Combine all ingredients except the olive or lemon twist in a mixing glass with ice. Stir well and strain into the serving glass. Garnish with the olive or lemon twist.

Gin and It

Serve in a chilled cocktail glass.

1 oz. gin

1 oz. sweet vermouth

Combine all ingredients in a mixing glass with ice. Stir well and strain into the serving glass.

Sweet Martini

Serve in a chilled cocktail glass.

2 oz. gin

$^1/_2$ oz. sweet vermouth

Dash orange bitters

Orange peel

Combine all ingredients except the orange peel in a mixing glass with ice. Stir well and strain into the serving glass. Twist the orange peel over the drink and garnish.

Chapter 6

Bourbon and Whiskey

In This Chapter

➤ Bourbon vs. Tennessee whiskey

➤ How to enjoy whiskey neat

➤ Bourbon and whiskey recipes

"The United States is the world's largest producer and consumer of whiskey," the *Encyclopedia Britannica*'s article on "whiskey" concludes matter-of-factly. But the numbers are anything but matter of fact: Americans have more than *500 brands* of the great American whiskey, bourbon, to choose from. How many other products can you think of that are offered in 500 brands?

Nor is there any product more American than bourbon. It is rooted in colonial times and was among the very first of American industries. It was also among the first products the Feds hit on as a source of tax revenue. And *that* practically caused a war.

This chapter will tell you what all the fuss has been about for all these years.

Bar Tips

The cowpoke thrusts aside the swinging saloon doors, moseys up to the bar, orders a shot of whiskey, and downs it in a gulp. You can do this, too. But why waste *really good* whiskey? Fine whiskey, like fine wine, is meant to be savored and is best enjoyed slowly.

Neat, Rocks, Branch, Soda

Really good whiskey is a pleasure to enjoy neat (straight, no ice, no water), on the rocks, with club soda, or with what Southerners like to call *branch* or *branch water*, which, these days, is just tap water.

What do you need to know about enjoying whiskey unadorned? A little:

1. Invest in a premium-label bourbon or Tennessee whiskey. With some 500 brands, you have a lot of sampling to do.

2. Generally speaking, higher-proof whiskies are best for sipping.

3. Use scrupulously clean and thoroughly rinsed glassware.

4. Use ice that is free from freezer burn and freezer odors and tastes. Commercial bagged ice is best.

5. If your tap water tastes good, use it. Otherwise, consider bottled spring water. If you are *really* serious about sampling a variety of whiskies, use distilled water, which is the most neutral mixer available.

6. If you want effervescence, you can mix your whiskey with club soda, soda water, seltzer, or unflavored sparkling water, such as Perrier. If you want the most neutral carbonated mixer, use soda water.

Juleps: The Schools of Thought

As the subject of the martini sparks debate in the cold North, so, in the sunny South, the Mint Julep is a source of many genteelly heated and arcane discussions. Three juleps that claim to be "standard" follow.

Mint Julep Version 1
Serve in an old-fashioned glass.

$1/2$ tsp. fine-grained sugar

$2^1/2$ oz. bourbon

Splash club soda

Mint sprig

Put the $1/2$ teaspoon of sugar in the bottom of the mixing glass. Fill the glass one-third full with ice cubes. Add bourbon. Add the splash of club soda. Garnish with the mint sprig.

Mint Julep 2
Serve in a Collins glass.

2 oz. bourbon

6 mint leaves

$1/2$ oz. sugar syrup

Mint sprig

Place the mint leaves in the bottom of the serving glass and add the sugar syrup. Mash the leaves in the syrup. Add half the bourbon, then fill the glass with crushed ice. Add the balance of the bourbon and stir vigorously. Garnish with the mint sprig.

Mint Julep 3

Serve in an old-fashioned or Collins glass.

1 cube sugar

3 oz. bourbon

Mint sprigs

Dissolve the sugar cube in the bottom of the serving glass with a few drops of plain water. Add a few mint sprigs. Fill the glass with ice (cubes or crushed) then add the bourbon. Stir well. Cut up some more mint sprigs and add these to the drink. Stir, then allow to stand several minutes before serving.

Frozen Julep

Serve in a large (double) old-fashioned glass.

2 oz. bourbon	6 small mint leaves
1 oz. lemon juice	Mint sprig
1 oz. sugar syrup	

In a mixing glass, muddle the mint leaves together with the bourbon, lemon juice, and sugar syrup. Put the muddled ingredients in a blender with crushed ice. Blend until ice becomes mushy. Pour into the serving glass and garnish with a mint sprig.

Buzzed Words

To **muddle** is to mash and stir. Mint leaves and other solids are muddled in order to make a suspension or a paste with fluid. A special pestle-like wooden **muddler** can be used to muddle, but any spoon will do.

The Classic Bourbon and Tennessee Cocktails

You can use bourbon or Tennessee whiskey to make any of the recipes in this chapter. Throughout, we've called for "bourbon"; add the equivalent amount of Tennessee whiskey if you prefer. For the more strongly flavored drinks, there is no reason to splurge on premium-label whiskey. Ordinary "bar bourbon" will do just fine.

Bluegrass Cocktail

Serve in a chilled cocktail glass.

1^1/$_2$ oz. bourbon

1 oz. pineapple juice

1 oz. lemon juice

1 tsp. maraschino liqueur

Combine all ingredients in a shaker with ice. Shake vigorously, then strain into the serving glass.

Strictly speaking, a *cobbler* is an iced drink made with wine or liqueur plus sugar and fruit juice; however, no one is likely to complain if you throw in some bourbon. Beware. Like the Mint Julep, this is a potent blend. Sugar and carbonated water speed the absorption of alcohol into the bloodstream. The drink goes down so easily that you and your guests will be tempted to gulp. Sip! Please!

Bourbon Cobbler

Serve in a chilled highball glass.

1¹/₂ oz. bourbon	1 tsp. sugar syrup
1 oz. Southern Comfort	Club soda to fill
1 tsp. peach-flavored brandy	Peach slice
2 tsp. lemon juice	

Combine all ingredients except the club soda and the peach slice in a shaker with cracked ice. Shake vigorously, then pour into the serving glass. Add several ice cubes, then the club soda to fill. Garnish with the peach slice.

Made with the traditional gin, it's called a Tom Collins. With bourbon, some call it a John Collins—a nod, doubtless, to the spirit of John Barleycorn, traditional personification of alcohol. You can have yours relatively subdued or jet-assisted, with higher-proof bourbon and a Peychaud's send-off.

Bourbon Collins (Unadorned)

Serve in a chilled Collins glass.

1 oz. bourbon

¹/₂ oz. lime juice

1 tsp. sugar syrup

Club soda to fill

Lime peel

Combine all ingredients except lime peel and club soda in a shaker with cracked ice. Shake vigorously, then pour into the serving glass. Add club soda to fill and garnish with the lime peel.

Bourbon Collins (Augmented)

Serve in a chilled highball glass.

2 oz. 100-proof bourbon

$1/2$ oz. lemon juice

1 tsp. sugar syrup

Few dashes of Peychaud's bitters

Club soda to fill

Lemon slice

Combine all ingredients except the lemon slice and club soda in a shaker with cracked ice. Shake vigorously, then pour into the serving glass. Add club soda to fill and garnish with the lemon slice.

Bourbon Manhattan

Serve in a chilled cocktail glass.

2 oz. bourbon

$1/2$ oz. sweet vermouth

Dash Angostura or other bitters

Maraschino cherry

Combine all ingredients except the cherry in a mixing glass with ice. Stir well, then strain into the serving glass. Garnish with the cherry.

Bourbon Old-Fashioned
Serve on the rocks in an old-fashioned glass.

$1^1/_2$ oz. bourbon

Splash of water

Dash sugar syrup

Liberal dash Angostura bitters

Combine all ingredients over ice in the serving glass. Stir well.

Bourbon Rose (Dark)
Serve in a chilled highball glass.

$1^1/_2$ oz. bourbon   4 oz. orange juice

1 oz. triple sec   Grenadine

Combine all ingredients except grenadine in a shaker with cracked ice. Shake vigorously, then pour into the serving glass. *Carefully* pour a float of grenadine on top. Do not stir.

Bourbon Rose (Pale)
Serve in a chilled old-fashioned glass.

$1^1/_2$ oz. bourbon

$1/_2$ oz. dry vermouth

$1/_2$ oz. crème de cassis

$1/_2$ oz. lemon juice

Combine all ingredients in a shaker with cracked ice. Shake vigorously, then pour into the serving glass.

Bourbon Sidecar
Serve in a chilled cocktail glass.

1$^1/_2$ oz. bourbon

$^3/_4$ oz. curaçao or triple sec

$^1/_2$ oz. lemon juice

Combine all ingredients in a shaker with cracked ice. Shake vigorously, then strain into the serving glass.

Bourbon Sour
Serve in a chilled Sour glass.

2 oz. bourbon

Juice of $^1/_2$ lemon

$^1/_2$ tsp. sugar syrup

Orange slice

Maraschino cherry

Combine all ingredients except the fruit in a shaker with ice. Shake vigorously, then strain into the serving glass. Garnish with the fruit.

New Traditions

Bourbon has a not entirely undeserved reputation as a man's drink—or, more precisely, an "old boy's drink." It summons up visions of conservative gentlemen reading their papers in darkly paneled club rooms thick with cigar smoke. The following are some recipes designed to update the bourbon profile.

While most committed bourbon drinkers shy away from scotch, they usually enjoy gin well enough and have been known to down the occasional martini. Behold—the Dry Mahoney!

Dry Mahoney
Serve in a chilled cocktail glass.

$2^1/_2$ oz. bourbon

$^1/_2$ oz. dry vermouth

Lemon twist

Combine all ingredients except the lemon twist in a mixing glass filled with ice. Stir vigorously, then strain into the serving glass. Garnish with the lemon twist. It is recommended that the drink be served with a few ice cubes on the side, in a second glass.

Millionaire Cocktail
Serve in chilled cocktail glasses.

3 oz. bourbon	Few dashes grenadine
1 oz. Pernod	1 egg white *
Few dashes curaçao	

Combine all ingredients in a mixing glass with cracked ice. Stir well, and strain into the serving glasses. *Recipe makes two drinks.*

* Raw egg may be a source of salmonella bacteria. You may wish to avoid drinks calling for raw egg yolk or white.

What is the origin of the name of the following drink? We have so far failed to discern the religious significance of combining ginger ale with club soda. Still, it's a pretty good drink.

Presbyterian
Serve on the rocks in a highball glass.

3 oz. bourbon

Equal portions of ginger ale and

Club soda to fill

Pour bourbon into serving glass half filled with ice cubes. Add equal portions of ginger ale and club soda to fill.

Bar Tips
Most drinks that call for egg white require half an egg white. But it's almost impossible to get *half* an egg white; therefore, all recipes in this book calling for egg white make *two* drinks.

Simple Sazerac
Serve in a chilled old-fashioned glass.

$^1/_4$ tsp. Pernod or other absinthe substitute

$^1/_2$ tsp. sugar

1 tbsp. water

Dash Peychaud's bitters

2 oz. bourbon (may also use rye or blended whiskey)

Lemon peel

Coat the serving glass by swirling the Pernod in it. Add the sugar, water, and Peychaud's. Muddle these until the sugar is completely dissolved. Add bourbon with a few ice cubes. Stir vigorously. Garnish with the lemon peel.

Buzzed Words

Absinthe is an aromatic, bitter, very strong liqueur flavored chiefly with wormwood and other botani-cals. Absinthe was outlawed in many countries early in the 20th century because of its apparent toxicity.

Now, except for the absinthe, here is the original Sazerac. You'll need two old-fashioned glasses. Herbsaint is an absinthe stand-in that may be hard to find outside of New Orleans; you may substitute Pernod.

Original Sazerac

Serve in a chilled old-fashioned glass.

1 sugar cube

2 dashes Peychaud's bitters

Dash Angostura bitters

2 oz. 100-proof bourbon (may substitute rye or blended whiskey)

Dash Herbsaint (may substitute Pernod)

Lemon peel

Use crushed ice to chill *two* old-fashioned glasses. Pour out the ice from one glass. In the bottom of that glass put the sugar cube with a few drops of water. Add the bitters, and muddle the sugar and bitters until the sugar is dissolved. Add bourbon and ice cubes. Stir well. Empty the second glass of ice and add a liberal dash of Herbsaint, swirling to coat the glass. Discard the excess bitters and pour in the mixture from the first glass. Twist the lemon peel over the glass, but *do not garnish with the lemon peel*; discard.

Ward Eight
Serve in a chilled cocktail glass.

2 oz. bourbon

1 oz. lemon juice

1 oz. orange juice

Sugar syrup to taste

Dash grenadine

Combine all ingredients in a shaker with ice. Shake vigorously and strain into the serving glass.

Chapter 7

Canadian and American Whiskeys

In This Chapter

➤ How blended whiskey is made

➤ Why blended whiskey is a great mixer

➤ How to select a blended whiskey

➤ Blended whiskey recipes

Americans tend to enjoy a lighter beverage than Europeans; for example, in the United States, ale and stout have never been as popular as beer. So it is with whiskey. To be sure, many Americans like their bourbon and scotch, but blended whiskey is a North American phenomenon, a beverage that is less filling and lighter in body than bourbon, scotch, or rye. Some of the most popular U.S. and Canadian whiskies are blended. They make great mixers, as you'll see.

The Master Blender at Work

Blended whiskies may combine various straight whiskies (whiskies distilled from the mash of a single grain) only, or may involve combinations of straight, mixed-grain whiskies, grain neutral spirits, and so-called *light whiskies*. The latter are whiskies distilled at high proof—over 160—and stored in used charred oak barrels. The result is more flavorful than neutral spirits, but not as strong as straight whiskey. In a blend, light whiskey imparts character without compromising the light, dry quality desired in a blend.

The creation of a fine blended whiskey is as much art as science; a *master blender* directs the creation of a blended whiskey. The blender may combine as many as 50 whiskies drawn from a "library" of hundreds of products.

Buzzed Words

Straight whiskey is made from mash containing at least 51 percent of a certain grain; however, straight corn whiskey mash contains 80 percent corn. With **mixed-grain whiskies**, no single grain predominates. **Light whiskey** is distilled in excess of 160 proof and aged in charred oak barrels. An important component in blended whiskey, it is more flavorful than neutral spirits, but not as strong as straight whiskey.

Not "Whiskey," but "Whisky": Enjoying the Canadian Difference

So far as the quality of lightness goes, the Canadian distillers of blended whisky (that's how Canadians spell it) have taken the beverage to its extreme. Light, delicately flavored, and extremely smooth, Canadian whiskies are ideal mixers.

Neat, Rocks, Soda, Ginger

You'll want to devote a good deal of pleasurable effort to discovering your favorite blends, particularly if you intend to enjoy the whiskey neat, on the rocks, or with plain soda. Soapy glasses, chlorine-laden tap water, or freezer-burned ice will spoil the taste of delicately flavored American and Canadian blends.

Ginger ale has always been a popular mixer with blended whiskey. Just pour a jigger of whiskey into a highball glass filled with ice and add ginger ale to fill. If you want something a little fancier and quite a bit stronger, try the Horse's Neck.

Buzzed Words

The **master blender** is the craftsperson in charge of selecting and proportioning the component whiskies that make up a blended whiskey.

Manhattan Varieties

The woodwind tones of a good blended or Canadian whiskey are perfectly suited to the Manhattan. Made carefully, the Manhattan is a delicate and subtle drink, despite its essential sweetness. While many people have theirs on the rocks, it is best enjoyed well-chilled, straight-up. The basic, unadorned recipe follows.

Manhattan
Serve in a chilled cocktail glass.

2 oz. blended whiskey   Dash Angostura bitters

1/2 oz. sweet vermouth   Maraschino cherry

Combine all ingredients except the cherry with ice in a mixing glass. Stir well, then strain into the serving glass and garnish with the cherry.

Dry Manhattan
Serve in a chilled cocktail glass.

2 oz. blended whiskey

1/2 oz. dry vermouth

Dash Angostura bitters (optional)

Lemon twist

Combine all ingredients except the lemon twist with ice in a mixing glass. Stir well, then strain into the serving glass and garnish with the lemon twist.

Old-Fashioned Manhattan
Serve in a chilled cocktail glass.

1 1/2 blended whiskey

1 1/2 oz. sweet vermouth

Maraschino cherry

Combine ingredients except the cherry in a shaker with cracked ice. Shake vigorously, then pour into the serving glass and garnish with the cherry.

Perfect Manhattan

Serve in a chilled cocktail glass.

2 oz. blended whiskey

$^1/_2$ oz. sweet vermouth

$^1/_4$ oz. dry vermouth

Dash Angostura bitters

Maraschino cherry

Combine all ingredients except the cherry in a mixing glass with ice. Stir well, then strain into the serving glass and garnish with the cherry.

Bar Tips

You can make the recipes in this chapter with American or Canadian blended whiskey; however, at the end of the chapter you'll find a group of recipes in which the ultra-light Canadian product works best.

Fizzes

Blended whiskey is the perfect choice among the "dark spirits" for fizz drinks because its light qualities complement effervescence and don't fight sweet mixers.

Whiskey Curaçao Fizz
Serve in a chilled Collins glass.

2 oz. blended whiskey   1 tsp. sugar
1/2 oz. curaçao   Club soda to fill
1 oz. lemon juice   Orange slice

Combine all ingredients except the orange slice and club soda in a shaker with cracked ice. Shake well, then pour into the serving glass. You may add additional ice cubes, if you wish. Add club soda to fill. Garnish with the orange slice.

Whiskey Fizz
Serve in a chilled highball glass.

1 1/2 oz. blended whiskey   1/2 tsp. sugar syrup
Few dashes Angostura bitters   Club soda to fill

Combine all ingredients except the club soda in the serving glass one third full of ice. Stir well, then add club soda to fill.

Grapefruit Combos
While the combination of bourbon or scotch with grapefruit juice may raise some eyebrows, the cleaner, lighter taste of blended whiskey makes it all seem perfectly natural.

Grapefruit Cooler
Serve in a chilled Collins glass.

2 oz. blended whiskey   1/4 oz. lemon juice
4 oz. grapefruit juice   1/2 orange slice
1/2 oz. red currant syrup   1/2 lemon slice

Combine all ingredients except the fruit in a shaker with cracked ice. Pour into the serving glass, adding ice cubes, if you wish. Garnish with the orange and lemon.

Old-Fashioneds and a Rickey

Blended Whiskey Old-Fashioned
Serve on the rocks in an old-fashioned glass.

1¹/₂ oz. blended whiskey

Dash water

Dash sugar syrup

Liberal dash Angostura bitters

Combine all ingredients in a serving glass half full of ice.

Canadian Old-Fashioned
Serve in a chilled old-fashioned glass.

1¹/₂ oz. Canadian whisky	Dash Angostura bitters
¹/₂ tsp. curaçao	Lemon twist
Dash lemon juice	Orange twist

Combine all ingredients except twists in a shaker with cracked ice. Shake vigorously, then pour into the serving glass. Garnish with the twists.

Whiskey Rickey
Serve on the rocks in a Collins glass.

1¹/₂ oz. blended whiskey	Club soda to fill
Juice of ¹/₂ lime	Lime twist
1 tsp. sugar syrup	

Combine all ingredients except the lime twist and club soda in the serving glass at least half filled with ice. Stir well. Add club soda to fill and garnish with the lime twist.

Pucker Up

Whiskey Sour
Serve in a chilled sour glass.

2 oz. blended whiskey   Maraschino cherry

1 oz. sour mix   Orange slice

Combine all ingredients except fruit in a shaker with cracked ice. Shake vigorously. Pour into the serving glass and garnish with fruit.

Alternative Whiskey Sour
Serve in a chilled sour glass.

2 oz. blended whiskey   Maraschino cherry

1 oz. lemon juice   Orange slice

1 tbs. sugar syrup

Combine all ingredients except fruit in a shaker with cracked ice. Shake vigorously. Pour into the serving glass and garnish with fruit.

On the Sweet Side

New Yorker
Serve in a chilled cocktail glass.

$1^1/_2$ oz. blended whiskey   Dash grenadine

$^1/_2$ oz. lime juice   Lemon twist

1 tsp. sugar syrup   Orange twist

Combine all ingredients except fruit in a shaker with ice. Shake vigorously, then pour into the serving glass and garnish with the twists.

Buzzed Words

A **daisy** is a whiskey- or gin-based drink that includes some sweet syrup and a float of (usually golden) liqueur.

Whiskey Daisy

Serve in a chilled highball glass.

2 oz. blended whiskey

1 tsp. red currant syrup (may also use raspberry syrup or grenadine)

$1/2$ oz. lemon juice

Club soda to fill (optional)

1 tsp. yellow Chartreuse (or other light liqueur)

Lemon slice

Combine all ingredients except liqueur, club soda, and lemon slice in a shaker with cracked ice. Shake vigorously and pour into the serving glass. Carefully add the liqueur for a float. Do not stir. Garnish with the lemon slice.

Black Hawk

Serve in a chilled cocktail glass.

1 oz. blended whiskey	$1/2$ oz. lemon juice
1 oz sloe gin	Maraschino cherry

Combine all ingredients except the cherry in a shaker with ice. Shake vigorously and strain into the serving glass. Garnish with the maraschino cherry.

Toast

May you live forever, and may I never die.

7&7
Serve on the rocks in a highball glass.

1¹/₂ oz. Seagram's 7-Crown

4 oz. 7-Up

Pour the whiskey into the serving glass filled with ice. Add 7-Up.

With Wines and Liqueurs

Ladies' Cocktail
Serve in a chilled cocktail glass.

1¹/₂ oz. blended whiskey

1 tsp. anisette

Few dashes Pernod

Few dashes Angostura bitters

Pineapple stick

Combine all ingredients except the pineapple stick in a shaker with cracked ice. Shake vigorously and strain into the serving glass. Garnish with the pineapple stick.

Madeira Cocktail

Serve in a chilled old-fashioned glass.

1¹/₂ oz. blended whiskey   Dash lemon juice

1¹/₂ oz. Malmsey Madeira   Orange slice

1 tsp. grenadine

Combine all ingredients except the orange slice in a shaker with cracked ice. Shake vigorously and pour into the serving glass. Garnish with the orange slice.

O, Canada!

All of the recipes in this chapter can be made with Canadian whisky instead of American blended whiskey, if you prefer. But here are a few drinks especially for Canadian whisky.

Dog Sled

Serve in a chilled old-fashioned glass.

2 oz. Canadian whisky   1 tbsp. lemon juice

2 oz. orange juice   1 tsp. grenadine

Combine all ingredients with cracked ice in a shaker. Shake vigorously, then pour into the serving glass.

Frontenac Cocktail

Serve in a chilled cocktail glass.

1¹/₂ oz. Canadian whisky   Few dashes kirsch

¹/₂ oz. Grand Marnier   Dash orange bitters

Combine all ingredients with cracked ice in a shaker. Shake vigorously, then pour into the serving glass.

Saskatoon Stinger

Serve on the rocks in an old-fashioned glass.

2 oz. Canadian whisky

1 oz. peppermint schnapps (may substitute white crème de menthe)

Lemon twist

Pour the whisky and schnapps into the serving glass half filled with ice cubes. Stir well, and garnish with the lemon twist.

Chapter 8

Comin' Through the Rye

In This Chapter

➤ Why rye is a "drinker's drink"
➤ Where rye comes from
➤ A good reason to avoid cheap rye
➤ Rye recipes

Rye is one of those spirits people call a "drinker's drink," which means that a lot of folks just don't like the stuff. It does come on strong, but if you like scotch, rye is worth giving a chance. This chapter has some suggestions for enjoying this black sheep among whiskies.

The Black Sheep

Rye is a cereal grain that has been cultivated at least since 6500 B.C. Despite its lengthy lineage, it's always been something of a second-class grain, grown mainly where the climate and soil are unfavorable for other, more favored cereals, or cultivated as a winter crop in places too cold to grow winter wheat. You can make a loaf of bread with rye, but, even here, it doesn't measure up to wheat because it lacks the requisite elasticity. The rye bread most of us eat is almost always a blend of rye and wheat;

traditionally, black bread, made entirely from rye, has been associated with poverty (though the moderately increasing popularity of pumpernickel in the United States has upgraded the stature of rye grain somewhat).

So there it is: the rather sad story of this hearty, but hardpressed cereal grain. And it gets sadder.

Bar Tips

Rye has fallen so far out of the loop that drinkers who ask for "rye and ginger," are probably expecting to be served a blended whiskey with ginger ale. Respond to the request thus—"Do you want rye or blended whiskey?"

Rye, Unadorned

The fact is, rye offers a full-bodied, up-and-at-'em alternative to scotch and Irish whiskey, the two whiskey types it most resembles in flavor. Invest in a good rye. Cheap brands give new meaning to the term *rotgut* and are characterized by a musty taste—like sipping something that's been sitting in a damp basement for far too long. Drinking rye should not be a punishment. In many liquor stores, you'll find but a single premium brand, Old Overholt, the most widely marketed rye. Fortunately, it's quite good.

Rock and Rye: What It Is and What to Do with It

Rock and rye is not rye whiskey on the rocks. It is a liqueur, marketed under various brand names, made with rye whiskey, whole fruits—you'll see them in the bottle—and rock candy. Since every time you say *rye*, the phrase "rock and rye" will jump up like a leg whose knee has been tapped by a rubber mallet, you'd better know what to do with rock and rye.

Basically, there are two things you can do. You can make a *cooler* or you can make a *heater*.

Rock and Rye Cooler
Serve in a highball glass.

1¹/₂ oz. vodka
1 oz. rock and rye
2 tsp. lime juice

Lemon-lime soda to fill
Lime slice

Combine all ingredients except soda in a shaker with ice. Shake vigorously, then strain into the serving glass half filled with ice cubes. Add lemon-lime soda to fill and garnish with a lime slice.

Rock and Rye Toddy
Serve in a heat-proof mug.

2 oz. rock and rye
3 oz. boiling water
2 dashes Angostura bitters

Lemon slice
Cinnamon stick
Grated nutmeg

Combine rock and rye with bitters in the mug. Drop in the lemon slice, then pour on boiling water. Garnish with the cinnamon stick and grated nutmeg.

Certain old-timers swear by the Rock and Rye Toddy as very comforting to cold sufferers. We make absolutely no claim to any health benefits, but just pass on this fragment of folk wisdom.

Buzzed Words
A **toddy** is a hot drink consisting of liquor (often rum), water, sugar, and spices.

Fizz and Flip

A *fizz* is just about any drink made with sugar and soda, and a *flip* is a drink with liquor, sugar, spice, and egg. Both have pleasantly old-fashioned qualities, which make them perfect for rye, itself an old-fashioned spirit.

Rye Fizz

Serve on the rocks in a highball glass.

1¹/₂ oz. rye	Dash sugar syrup
Dash Angostura bitters	Club soda to fill

Combine all ingredients except the soda in a mixing glass. Stir well and pour into the serving glass filled with ice. Add club soda to fill.

Bar Tip

The best way to chill a brandy snifter is with crushed ice. Pour it into the snifter, allow the snifter to chill, then pour out the ice when you are ready to pour in the drink. Putting a delicate snifter in a refrigerator or freezer may crack it.

Rye Flip

Serve in a chilled brandy snifter.

1¹/₂ oz. rye	1 tsp. sugar syrup
1 egg *	Ground nutmeg

Combine all ingredients except nutmeg in a shaker with ice. Shake vigorously, then strain into the serving glass. Sprinkle with nutmeg.

* Raw egg may be a source of salmonella bacteria. You may wish to avoid drinks calling for raw egg yolk or white.

Hesitation
Serve in a chilled cocktail glass.

1^1/$_2$ oz. rye

1^1/$_2$ oz. Swedish punsch

Few liberal dashes lemon juice

Combine all ingredients in a shaker with cracked ice. Shake vigorously, then pour into the serving glass.

Hunter's Cocktail
Serve on the rocks in an old-fashioned glass.

1^1/$_2$ oz. rye

^{1}/$_2$ oz. cherry brandy

Maraschino cherry

Combine rye and brandy over ice in the serving glass. Stir, then garnish with the cherry.

Lisbon Cocktail
Serve in chilled old-fashioned glasses.

3 oz. rye	2 tsp. sugar syrup
4 oz. port	1 egg white *
1 oz. lemon juice	

Combine all ingredients in a shaker with cracked ice. Shake vigorously, then pour into the serving glasses. *Recipe makes two drinks.*

* Raw egg may be a source of salmonella bacteria. You may wish to avoid drinks calling for raw egg yolk or white.

Citrus Varieties

Bal Harbour is a Florida coastal community so upscale that it had to spell its name the British way. Its namesake cocktail smacks of easy living among old money.

Bal Harbour Cocktail
Serve in a chilled cocktail glass.

1¹/₂ oz. rye	1 oz. grapefruit juice
¹/₂ oz. dry vermouth	Maraschino cherry

Combine all ingredients except the cherry in a shaker with cracked ice. Shake vigorously, then strain into the serving glass. Garnish with the maraschino cherry.

With Liqueurs and Bitters

Rye really comes into its own when combined with liqueurs and bitters. These drinks are decidedly not for people who want a "lite" experience. They'll take you the whole nine yards.

Frisco Cocktail
Serve in a chilled cocktail glass.

1¹/₂ oz. rye	¹/₂ oz. lemon juice
1¹/₂ oz. Benedictine	Orange twist

Combine all ingredients except the orange twist in a shaker with ice. Shake vigorously, then strain into the serving glass and garnish with the twist.

Lord Baltimore's Cup
Serve in a chilled large wine glass or wine goblet.

$1/2$ tsp. sugar syrup   Champagne to fill

Few dashes Angostura bitters   1 tsp. Pernod for float

1 oz. rye

Combine the sugar and bitters in the serving glass. Add rye, along with several ice cubes, then fill with champagne. Carefully add Pernod as a float. Do not stir.

Pink Rye
Serve on the rocks in an old-fashioned glass.

$1^1/2$ oz. rye

Liberal dashes Angostura syrup

Combine the ingredients in the serving glass filled with ice. Stir well.

Rye Manhattans
The versatile Manhattan can be made with bourbon, blended whiskey, scotch, and rye. The basic recipe follows.

Rye Manhattan
Serve in a chilled cocktail glass.

$1^1/2$ oz. rye

$1/4$ oz. sweet vermouth

Maraschino cherry

Combine the rye and vermouth in a mixing glass filled with ice. Stir well, then strain into the serving glass and garnish with the cherry.

Dry Rye Manhattan

Serve in a chilled cocktail glass.

1 1/2 oz. rye

1/4 oz. dry vermouth

Maraschino cherry

Combine the rye and vermouth in a mixing glass filled with ice. Stir well, then strain into the serving glass and garnish with the cherry.

Perfect Rye Manhattan

Serve in a chilled cocktail glass.

2 oz. rye   Few dashes Agnostura bitters

1/2 tsp. sweet vermouth   Maraschino cherry

1/2 tsp. dry vermouth

Combine all ingredients except cherry in a shaker with ice. Shake vigorously, then strain into the serving glass and garnish with the cherry.

Quick One

Commuter to train conductor: "This morning I accidentally left a small bottle of rye on the train. Was it turned into the Lost-and-Found?"

"No," the conductor replied, "but the guy who found it was."

Bar Tips

Drinks calling for egg white generally require half an egg white, but since it is almost impossible to separate half an egg white from a whole one, the smart thing is to make two drinks.

Elk's Own

Serve in a chilled old-fashioned glass.

1½ oz. rye	1 egg white
¾ oz. port	1 tsp. powdered sugar
Juice of ½ lemon	Pineapple stick

Combine all ingredients except the pineapple stick in a shaker with cracked ice. Shake vigorously, then pour into the serving glass and garnish with the pineapple stick.

Indian River Rye Cocktail

Serve in a chilled old-fashioned glass.

1 oz. rye	2 oz. orange juice
1 oz. dry vermouth	Few dashes raspberry syrup

Combine all ingredients in a shaker with cracked ice. Shake vigorously, then pour into the serving glass.

Toast

Here's to you and here's to me. And here's to love and laughter. I'll be true as long as you. But not a minute after.

Chapter 9

Scotch Snobs and Irish Spirits

In This Chapter

➤ How scotch is made
➤ Scotch vs. Irish whiskey
➤ Scotch recipes

Of all distilled spirits, scotch comes closest to wine in terms of commanding a legion of connoisseurs both dedicated and disputatious. Like making wine, creating scotch is theoretically quite simple. There is fermentation, distilling, aging, then bottling. In the case of blended scotch, there is the added complication of blending 15 to 50 whiskies. Yet, still, as the saying goes, this isn't rocket science. Nevertheless, scotch varies greatly in taste from label to label, and just why this is the case is a subject of deep mystery.

As to Irish whiskey, its following is much smaller than the host of scotch fanciers; yet, thanks to the great popularity of a number of liqueurs based on Irish whiskey (paramountly Irish Mist and Bailey's Original Irish Cream), the whiskey itself is enjoying increasing demand in the United States. It's certainly worth trying.

The casual scotch drinker may or may not be familiar with the distinction between malt and grain whiskies, but all except the absolute neophyte have heard something about *single-malt* versus blended scotches.

Buzzed Words

Malt is grain (usually barley) that has been allowed to sprout.

Despite the effort that goes into creating blended scotch, it is much less expensive than single-malt scotch, which, despite growing American popularity, accounts for a scant two percent of scotch sales. As the name implies, single-malt scotch is made exclusively from malted barley, which means that it is aged at least 14 years. The whisky in a bottle of single-malt scotch has been distilled and aged during a single period and by a single distillery. The best-known names among the malted scotches ring out with Celtic grandeur: The Glenlivet, Knockando, Glenfiddich, Laphroaig, Glenmorangie, and Macallan.

Buzzed Words

Malt scotches are made entirely from malted barley and are distilled in relatively small pot stills. **Grain scotches** combine malted barley with unmalted barley and corn and are distilled in "continuous" stills.

Unmixed Pleasure: Neat, Rocks, Water, Soda

For the lover of fine scotch, few gustatorial pleasures exceed that of sampling the many blended and single-malt varieties available. Any of the premium-priced blended labels make for enjoyment, especially served on the rocks or with a plain mixer. The single-malt scotches are best-enjoyed neat—and absolutely *any* of these is sure to delight. Irish whiskey is likewise rewarding neat or on the rocks. Just remember the rules of enjoying fine whiskey in its unadorned state:

> ➤ Use super-clean glassware that is free from soap and detergent residue.

> ➤ Make certain any water that you add has no unwanted flavors or odors.

> ➤ Use the best ice possible. If you must take it from your freezer, run some water over it to get rid of freezer burn and any stray odors or flavors.

Classic Scotch Concoctions

Rob Roy
Serve in a chilled cocktail glass.

2 oz. scotch

$1/2$ oz. sweet vermouth

Maraschino cherry

Combine the scotch and sweet vermouth in a mixing glass with ice. Stir well, then strain into the serving glass and garnish with the cherry. For a Dry Rob Roy, substitute dry vermouth and garnish with a lemon twist. You'll find a variation in Appendix B.

This simple combination of scotch and scotch liqueur is among the most popular of scotch-based mixed drinks.

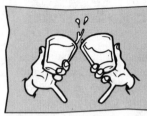

Toast

Women have many faults,
but men have only two:
everything they say and
everything they do!

Rusty Nail
Serve on the rocks in an old-fashioned glass.

1¹/₂ oz. scotch

1 oz. Drambuie

Combine ingredients in the serving glass half filled
with ice cubes. Stir. (If you prefer, the Drambuie can
be floated without stirring.)

Highland Fling with Milk
Serve in a chilled old-fashioned glass.

1¹/₂ oz. scotch   1 tsp. sugar syrup

3 oz. milk   Ground nutmeg

Combine all ingredients except nutmeg in a shaker
with cracked ice. Shake vigorously, then pour into the
serving glass and sprinkle with the nutmeg.

Highland Fling with Sweet Vermouth
Serve in a chilled cocktail glass.

1¹/₂ oz. scotch   Few dashes orange bitters

¹/₂ oz. sweet vermouth   Olive

Combine all ingredients except the olive in a shaker
with cracked ice. Shake vigorously, then strain into
the serving glass and garnish with the olive.

Quick One

Two men meet in a sleazy dockside bar.

"Lemme tell ya. It's gotten to the point where I get drunk mostly on water."

"That's crazy," the other man said. "Impossible!"

"It's a fact. Especially when you're cooped up with nothin' but men on the ship."

Scotch with Liqueurs

Scotch marries well with liqueurs, especially Drambuie, Scotland's immensely popular scotch-based liqueur.

Bairn

Serve in a chilled cocktail glass.

1¹/₂ oz. scotch

³/₄ oz. Cointreau

Few dashes orange bitters

Combine all ingredients in a shaker with ice. Shake vigorously, then pour into the serving glass.

Bar Tips

For mixed drinks, use blended scotch. There is no sane reason to expend the precious nectar of single-malt scotch in combination with strongly flavored mixers.

Blackwatch
Serve on the rocks in a highball glass.

1¹/₂ oz. scotch   Lemon slice
¹/₂ oz. curaçao   Mint sprig
¹/₂ oz. brandy

Combine all ingredients except the lemon slice and mint sprig in the serving glass half filled with ice cubes. Stir gently, then garnish with the lemon slice and mint sprig.

Dundee Dream
Serve in an old-fashioned glass.

1 oz. scotch   1 tsp. lemon juice
1 oz. gin   Lemon twist
¹/₂ oz. Drambuie   Maraschino cherry

Combine all ingredients except fruit in a shaker with cracked ice. Shake vigorously, then pour into the serving glass and garnish with the twist and cherry.

On the Sweet Side

Scotch is naturally the sweetest of whiskies and takes well to the more sugary mixers. The Scotch Orange Fix, for example, pairs scotch with sugar syrup and curaçao.

Scotch Sangaree
Serve in a large (double) old-fashioned glass.

1 tsp. heather honey   Club soda to fill
1¹/₂ oz. scotch   Grated nutmeg
Lemon twist

Mix the honey and a few splashes of the club soda in the serving glass. Stir until the honey is dissolved. Add the scotch and lemon twist, along with a few ice cubes. Stir. Add club soda to fill, and sprinkle with the nutmeg.

Smashes are drinks with loads of crushed ice.

Scotch Smash

Serve in a large (double) old-fashioned glass.

6 mint leaves

Heather honey (may substitute sugar syrup)

3 oz. scotch

Orange bitters

Muddle (mash and stir) the honey (or sugar syrup) with the mint leaves in the serving glass, then fill the glass with finely crushed ice. Add scotch and stir well. Dash on a topping of orange bitters and garnish with the mint sprig.

Vermouth Combinations

Blood and Sand

Serve in a chilled old-fashioned glass.

$^3/_4$ oz. scotch $^3/_4$ oz. sweet vermouth

$^3/_4$ oz. cherry brandy $^3/_4$ oz. orange juice

Combine all ingredients in a shaker with cracked ice. Shake vigorously, then pour into the serving glass.

Bobby Burns

Serve in a chilled cocktail glass.

$1^1/_2$ oz. scotch $^1/_2$ oz. sweet vermouth

$^1/_2$ oz. dry vermouth   Dash Benedictine

Combine all ingredients in a shaker with ice. Shake vigorously, then strain into the serving glass.

Brigadoon
Serve in a chilled old-fashioned glass.

1 oz. scotch

1 oz. grapefruit juice

1 oz. dry vermouth

Combine all ingredients in a shaker with cracked ice. Shake vigorously, then pour into the serving glass.

Liqueur and Aperitif Drinks

Blackthorn
Serve in a chilled old-fashioned glass.

1¹/₂ oz. Irish whiskey

1¹/₂ oz. dry vermouth

Liberal dashes Pernod

Liberal dashes Angostura bitters

Combine all ingredients in a shaker with cracked ice. Shake vigorously and pour into the serving glass.

Innisfree Fizz
Serve in a large wine glass or goblet.

2 oz. Irish whiskey

1 oz. lemon juice

1 oz. curaçao

¹/₂ tsp. sugar syrup

Club soda to fill

Combine all ingredients except the club soda in a shaker with ice. Shake vigorously, then strain into the serving glass and add club soda to fill.

Irish Rainbow

Serve in a chilled old-fashioned glass.

1^1/$_2$ oz. Irish whiskey

Liberal dashes Pernod

Liberal dashes curaçao

Liberal dashes maraschino liqueur

Liberal dashes Angostura bitters

Orange twist

Combine all ingredients except the twist in a shaker with cracked ice. Shake vigorously, then pour into the serving glass. Garnish with the orange twist.

Mists

Irish Mist is a highly popular and readily available liqueur based on Irish whiskey. Combined with more of its mother ingredient, it makes for some tempting whiskey-and-liqueur libations.

Ballylickey Belt

Serve in an old-fashioned glass.

^{1}/$_2$ tsp. heather honey	Club soda to fill
1^1/$_2$ oz. Irish whiskey	Lemon twist

Dissolve the honey with a few splashes of the club soda in the bottom of the serving glass. Add the whiskey and a few ice cubes, then club soda to fill. Garnish with the twist.

Irish Fix

Serve in a chilled old-fashioned glass.

2 oz. Irish whiskey

^{1}/$_2$ oz. Irish Mist

^{1}/$_2$ oz. lemon juice

^{1}/$_2$ oz. pineapple syrup (may substitute pineapple juice sweetened with a little sugar)

Orange slice

Lemon slice

Combine all ingredients except fruit in a shaker with cracked ice. Shake vigorously, then pour into the serving glass. Garnish with the fruit slices.

Sweet Drinks

Here is a nosegay of sweet drinks.

Bow Street Special

Serve in a chilled cocktail glass.

1^1/$_2$ oz. Irish whiskey

^{3}/$_4$ oz. triple sec

1 oz. lemon juice

Combine the ingredients in a shaker with cracked ice. Shake vigorously, then pour into the serving glass.

Grafton Street Sour

Serve in a chilled cocktail glass.

1¹/₂ oz. Irish whiskey   1 oz. lime juice

¹/₂ oz. triple sec   ¹/₄ oz. raspberry liqueur

Combine all ingredients except the raspberry liqueur in a shaker with ice. Shake vigorously, then strain into the serving glass. Carefully top with the liqueur.

Paddy Cocktail

Serve in a chilled cocktail glass.

1¹/₂ oz. Irish whiskey

³/₄ oz. sweet vermouth

Liberal dashes Angostura bitters

Combine the ingredients in a shaker with cracked ice. Shake vigorously, then pour into the serving glass.

Chapter 10

Caribbean Sugarcane: A Rum Résumé

In This Chapter

➤ Rum—a spirit of great variety
➤ The distinctive characters of rums from different countries
➤ Rums to drink straight and rums to mix
➤ Rum recipes

If you think of rum only as a clear, sweet liquor to mix with a Coke or throw into a daiquiri, you've got a vast tropical and semitropical world to explore. The fact is, even drinkers who are sophisticated in the nuances of bourbon and Tennessee whiskey and blended versus single-malt scotches often know very little about rum. It is produced in a dazzling variety of flavors in countries spanning the Caribbean and the Atlantic coast of Central and South America.

Buzzed Words

A **daiquiri** is a rum, lime juice, and sugar drink named after the Cuban town near the original Bacardi rum distillery.

So Near and Yet So Far

As with most spirits, the basic process of making rum is simple. Most rums are made from molasses, which is the residue that remains after sugar has been crystallized from sugarcane juice.

It is significant that the sugar necessary for fermentation is present in the molasses, which means that, more than any other distilled spirit, rum retains the flavor of the raw material from which it is made. This accounts in large part for the great variation in flavor and character among rums produced in different regions.

Another determinant of taste and character is the type of yeast employed to trigger the fermentation process. Each producer of rum closely guards its unique strain of yeast. Finally, distillation methods, aging duration and conditions, and blending also contribute to distinctive flavor. As with the blending of whiskey, the blending of rum is the work of a master blender, who tests, chooses, and combines the products of various distilleries and various ages to achieve a rum of distinctive character and consistent quality.

Buzzed Words

To **mull** a drink is to heat and spice it. Traditionally, the heating was done by inserting a hot poker into the drink; today, mulled drinks are usually heated on a stove.

Rum Solo

In general, the characteristic rums of Jamaica and the Demerara River region of Guyana are dark, heavy, and sweet. Barbados rums are golden or dark amber and neither as heavy nor as sweet as those of Jamaica or Demerara. Today, the characteristic rums of Puerto Rico and the Virgin Islands follow the pattern set by Bacardi in the mid-19th century in that they are dry and light. Long-aged rums—some of the best of which are produced in Colombia (Ron Medellin) and Venezuela (Cacique Ron Anejo)—take on a rich golden-amber color from the American Oak barrels in which they are stored for as much as 10 years.

Toast
May you have health, love, money, and time to spend it!

Bacardis

Bacardi
Serve in a chilled cocktail glass.

1¹/₂ oz. light or gold Bacardi rum

¹/₂ oz. lime juice

¹/₂ tsp. grenadine

Combine all ingredients in a shaker with cracked ice. Shake vigorously, then pour into the serving glass.

Bacardi Special

Serve in a chilled cocktail glass.

1¹/₂ oz. light Bacardi rum   ¹/₂ oz. lime juice

³/₄ oz. gin   ¹/₂ tsp. grenadine

Combine all ingredients in a shaker with cracked ice.
Shake vigorously, then pour into the serving glass.

Cuba Libre!

If you wish to reduce calories in the rum and Coke, use
diet cola. And if you want to add a touch of sophistication
to the drink, transform it into a Cuba Libre.

Cuba Libre

Serve on the rocks in a highball glass.

1¹/₂ oz. light or gold rum

Coca-Cola or other cola soft drink to fill

Lime wedge

Combine all ingredients except the lime in the serving
glass filled with ice. Garnish with the lime wedge.

No, you haven't misread the recipe: A Cuba Libre is a Rum
and Coke—garnished with a wedge of lime.

If you really want to transform this familiar drink into
something special, use dark rum and some cherry brandy
plus cola for the Cherry Cola.

Cherry Cola

Serve on the rocks in a lowball glass.

2 oz. dark rum

$^1/_2$ oz. cherry brandy

2 oz. Coca-Cola or other cola soft drink to fill

Lemon twist

Combine the ingredients in the serving glass filled with ice. Garnish with the twist.

Coladas

Pina Colada with Light Rum

Serve in a chilled Collins glass.

$1^1/_2$ oz. light rum	Splash cream
1 oz. cream of coconut	Maraschino cherry
2 oz. canned pineapple chunks	Orange slice
2 oz. pineapple juice	Pineapple stick

Combine all ingredients except fruit in a blender with 3 oz. of crushed ice. Blend until smooth, then pour into the serving glass and garnish with fruit.

Pina Colada with Gold Rum

Serve in a chilled Collins glass.

2 oz. gold rum	Pineapple stick
2 oz. cream of coconut	Maraschino cherry
4 oz. pineapple juice	

Combine all ingredients except fruit in a shaker with crushed ice. Shake vigorously, then pour into the serving glass. Garnish with fruit.

Daiquiris

Toast
To love and laughter and happily ever after!

Daiquiri
Serve in a chilled cocktail glass.

2 oz. light rum $^1/_2$ tsp. sugar syrup
Juice of $^1/_2$ lime   Orange slice

Combine all ingredients except the orange slice in a shaker with ice. Shake vigorously, then strain into the serving glass.

Daiquiri Dark
Serve in a chilled Collins glass.

2 oz. Jamaica rum $^1/_2$ tsp. sugar syrup
$^1/_2$ oz. lime juice

Combine all ingredients in a shaker with ice. Shake vigorously, then strain into the serving glass.

Bar Tips
Exotic rum drinks are best served in fun vessels—the kitschier the better. Comb flea markets and second-hand stores for Hurricane glasses, totem cups, and the like. Freely substitute these for the glassware recommended in this chapter.

Banana Daiquiri

Serve in a chilled cocktail glass.

1¹/₂ oz. light rum	1 tsp. sugar syrup
¹/₂ oz. lime juice	¹/₂ ripe banana, sliced

Combine all ingredients in a blender with cracked ice. Blend until smooth, then pour into the serving glass.

Strawberry Daiquiri

Serve in a chilled cocktail glass.

1¹/₂ oz. light rum

¹/₂ oz. lime juice

1 tsp. sugar syrup

6 large strawberries (fresh or frozen)

Combine all ingredients in a blender with cracked ice. Blend until smooth, then pour into the serving glass.

Peach Daiquiri

Serve in a chilled cocktail or wine glass.

2 oz. light rum	1 tsp. sugar syrup
¹/₂ oz. lime juice	¹/₂ oz. peach juice

Combine all ingredients in a blender with cracked ice. Blend until smooth, then pour into the serving glass.

Citrus Creations

Black Stripe
Serve in a chilled cocktail glass.

2 oz. dark Jamaica rum

1/2 oz. golden molasses

1/2 oz. lime juice

Combine all ingredients in a blender with cracked ice. Blend until smooth, then pour into the serving glass.

Buzzed Words

Grog was originally nothing more than rum diluted with water and rationed to sailors of the 18th-century Royal Navy. Its namesake was Admiral Edward Vernon (1684–1757), who first ordered the ration: Vernon's nickname was Old Grogram, after his habit of wearing a grogram (coarse wool) cloak.

Navy Grog
Serve in a chilled large (double) old-fashioned glass.

1 oz. light rum	1/2 oz. lime juice
1 oz. dark Jamaica rum	1/2 oz. pineapple juice
1 oz. 86-proof Demerara rum	1/2 oz. orgeat syrup
1/2 oz. orange juice	Lime slice
1/2 oz. guava juice	Mint sprig

Combine all ingredients except the lime slice and mint sprig in a shaker with cracked ice. Shake vigorously, then pour into the serving glass and garnish with the lime slice and mint sprig.

Zombie

Serve in a chilled Collins glass.

2 oz. light rum	1 oz. pineapple juice
1 oz. dark Jamaican rum	1/2 oz. papaya juice
1/2 oz. 151-proof Demerara rum	1/4 oz. grenadine
1 oz. curaçao	1/2 oz. orgeat syrup
1 tsp. Pernod	Mint sprig
1 oz. lemon juice	Pineapple stick
1 oz. orange juice	

Combine all ingredients except the pineapple stick and mint sprig in a blender with 3 oz. of cracked ice. Blend until smooth, then pour into the serving glass and garnish with the mint sprig and pineapple stick.

Island Hopping

Blue Hawaiian

Serve in a chilled Collins glass.

2 oz. light rum	1 oz. orange juice
1 oz. blue curaçao	1 oz. orange juice
1 oz. sour mix	1 oz. pineapple juice

Combine all ingredients in a blender with 3 oz. cracked ice. Blend until smooth, then pour into the serving glass.

Hurricane

Serve in a chilled cocktail glass.

1 oz. light rum	1/2 oz. passion fruit syrup
1 oz. gold rum	1/2 oz. lime juice

Combine all ingredients in a shaker with ice. Shake vigorously, then strain into the serving glass.

Toast

All that we have drank, sang, and danced, no one will ever take away from us.

Mai Tai

Serve in a chilled old-fashioned glass.

1 oz. Jamaica rum	$^1/_4$ oz. orgeat syrup
1 oz. Martinique rum	Lime twist
$^1/_2$ oz. curaçao	Mint sprig
$^1/_4$ oz. rock-candy syrup	Pineapple stick

Combine all ingredients except the twist, sprig, and stick in a shaker with cracked ice. Shake vigorously, then pour into the serving glass and garnish with the lime, mint, and pineapple.

Rum with Liqueurs and Brandy

Between the Sheets

Serve in a chilled cocktail glass.

$^3/_4$ oz. light rum	$^3/_4$ oz. Cointreau
$^3/_4$ oz. brandy	$^1/_2$ oz. lemon juice

Combine all ingredients with ice in a shaker. Shake vigorously, then strain into the serving glass.

Outrigger
Serve in a chilled cocktail glass.

1 oz. gold rum   1 oz. triple sec

1 oz. brandy $1/2$ oz. lime juice

Combine all ingredients in a shaker with ice. Shake vigorously, then strain into the serving glass.

Tiger's Milk
Serve in a chilled wine goblet.

$1^1/2$ oz. Bacardi Anejo gold rum   Sugar syrup to taste

$1^1/2$ oz. cognac   Grated nutmeg

4 oz. half-and-half

Combine all ingredients except nutmeg in a shaker with cracked ice. Shake vigorously, then pour into the serving glass. Dust with grated nutmeg.

Planter's Punch Variations

Planter's Punch is claimed as the property of the folks who make Myers's Rum. This is the recipe you'll find on a bottle of their dark rum.

The *Plantation* Punch throws Southern Comfort and brown sugar into the mix.

Planter's Punch
Serve in a chilled Collins glass.

2 oz. Myers's dark rum	Dash grenadine
3 oz. orange juice	Orange slice
Juice of 1/2 lemon or lime	Maraschino cherry
1 tsp. sugar	

Combine all ingredients except fruit in a shaker with cracked ice. Shake vigorously, then pour into the serving glass. Garnish with the orange slice and maraschino cherry.

Plantation Punch
Serve in a chilled Collins glass.

1 1/2 oz. dark Jamaica rum	Club soda to fill
3/4 oz. Southern Comfort	Orange slice
1 tsp. brown sugar	Lemon slice
1 oz. lemon juice	1 tsp. port

Combine all ingredients except club soda, fruit, and port in a shaker with cracked ice. Shake vigorously, then pour into the serving glass. Add club soda to fill and garnish with the fruit. Top off with the port.

Coffee Drinks

Jamaican coffee is also called a Calypso and makes a splendid after-dinner drink.

Jamaican Coffee (a.k.a. Calypso)
Serve in a coffee mug.

3/4 oz. Tia Maria	Hot coffee
3/4 oz. Jamaican rum	Whipped cream

Pour Tia Maria and rum into the mug and add coffee. Top with whipped cream.

Café Foster

1 oz. light or dark rum	Hot coffee
$^1/_2$ oz. crème de banana	Whipped cream

Pour rum and crème de banana into mug. Add coffee to fill, then top with whipped cream.

In addition to the many original mixed drinks featuring rum, the tropical spirit can stand in for a variety of liquors in familiar drinks. See Appendix B for all the rum variations of classics like the martini, the Collins, and the screwdriver.

Chapter 11

Tequila!

In This Chapter

➤ How to drink tequila, Pancho-Villa style

➤ The origin of tequila

➤ How tequila is made

➤ Tequila in white and gold

➤ Tequila recipes

Tequila—at least on the U.S. side of the border—has long been shrouded in disreputable myth. The truly callow still regard it as a hallucinogen—rendered particularly vile by the inclusion of a worm in the bottle—but, even among more sophisticated drinkers, tequila often has a reputation as a crude, harsh beverage redolent of raw yeast and industrial solvent.

The mistaken idea that tequila is a hallucinogen comes from confusing it with another spirit, *mescal*, which, like tequila, is made from the *agave* plant, albeit a different species. But all mescal shares with *mescaline*—a true hallucinogen—are the first two syllables. The origin of mescal is agave, whereas mescaline comes from *peyote*.

Tequila Varieties

Sample the various tequila brands imported into this country and choose your favorite. You should be aware of the two basic varieties, whatever the brand: the white tequila and the gold. White is unaged, bottled immediately after distillation. The gold, which sometimes shades into the brown range, called *tequila añejo*, is aged in oak casks. It acquires its color just as whiskey does, from the chemical interaction with the oak.

The difference between white tequila and *tequila añejo* is immediately apparent to the drinker. The aged product is much smoother and mellower, and the longer it has aged, the smoother and mellower it will be. It also costs more. White tequila is not a sipping drink. Either mix it or take it as a shooter, with salt and a lime wedge. *Tequila añejo*, however, may be mixed or savored slowly, like good whiskey or a fine cognac.

Buzzed Words

Tequila añejo is tequila that has been aged in oak casks, acquiring a gold coloring. Unaged tequila is clear and called **white** tequila.

Tequila Estilo Pancho Villa con Sangrita, Por Favor!

Okay, we've made such a fuss about Pancho Villa's version of a shooter, let's make with the details:

1. The tequila part is easy. Just pour a shot—a jigger—of white tequila in a shot glass.

2. Take a lime wedge between the thumb and forefinger of your left hand. (Unless you're left-handed. You're doing the shot with your good hand.)

3. Put a liberal pinch of coarse kitchen salt (not fine table salt) directly behind the held wedge, in the little hollow on the back of your hand between the base of your thumb and the base of your forefinger. (It helps to lick your hand first, so the salt stays put.)

4. Pick up the shot of tequila in your right hand.

5. Lick the salt, immediately down the tequila in a gulp, then suck the lime.

At this point, feel free to bang the bar several times as you struggle to resume respiration.

Alternatively, you may chase the shooter with *sangrita*, a traditional Mexican concoction without alcohol. Sangrita is available premixed in stores that specialize in Mexican foods, or you can mix your own:

Sangrita
Yields 3¹/₂ cups.

2 cups tomato juice

1 cup orange juice

2 oz. lime juice

2 tsp. Tabasco sauce (or to taste)

2 tsp. very finely minced onion

2 tsp. Worcestershire sauce (or to taste)

3 pinches white pepper

Pinch celery salt (to taste)

Combine all ingredients in a blender. Blend thoroughly, then strain into a container for chilling in the refrigerator.

Margarita

Serve in a chilled cocktail glass, optionally rimmed with coarse salt.

1¹/₂ oz. tequila (white or gold)

¹/₂ oz. triple sec

Juice of ¹/₂ large lime (or whole small lime)

Coarse salt

Lime slice

Combine all ingredients except the lime slice in a shaker with ice. Shake vigorously, then strain into the serving glass. Garnish with the lime slice.

Bar Tips

Traditionally, bartenders rim margarita glasses with coarse salt. (See Chapter 2 for information on how to rim a glass.) Many drinkers find a 50/50 mixture of salt and sugar more palatable. Try it.

Frozen Margarita

Serve in a large chilled cocktail glass or large chilled wine goblet rimmed with salt.

1¹/₂ oz. white tequila	Coarse salt
¹/₂ oz. triple sec	Lime slice
1 oz. lemon or lime juice	

Put approximately 2 cups of cracked ice in a blender. Add all ingredients except salt and lime slice. Blend until slushy. The mixture should be firm rather than watery. Pour into the serving glass. Garnish with the lime slice.

Frozen Fruit Margarita

Serve in a large, chilled cocktail glass or wine goblet rimmed with salt.

1½ oz. white tequila

½ oz. triple sec

½ oz. sour mix

Fresh fruit to taste

1 oz. fruit liqueur to harmonize with fresh fruit chosen

Dash Rose's lime juice

Coarse salt

Lime slice

Put approximately 2 cups of cracked ice in a blender. Add all ingredients except salt and lime slice. Blend until slushy. The mixture should be firm rather than watery. Pour into the serving glass. Garnish with lime slice.

Blue Margarita

Serve in a large, chilled cocktail glass or wine goblet rimmed with salt.

2 oz. white tequila

¾ oz. blue curaçao

2 oz. sour mix

½ oz. lime juice

Coarse salt

Lime slice

Combine all ingredients except salt and lime slice in a shaker with ice. Shake vigorously, then strain into the serving glass. Garnish with the lime slice.

Top-Shelf Margarita
Serve in a chilled cocktail glass rimmed with salt.

1½ oz. gold tequila   1 oz. lime juice

½ oz. Grand Marnier   Coarse salt

1 oz. sour mix   Lime slice

Combine all ingredients except the salt and lime slice in a shaker with ice. Shake vigorously, then strain into the serving glass. Garnish with the lime slice.

Sneaky Pete
Serve in a chilled cocktail glass.

2 oz. white tequila

½ oz. white crème de menthe

½ oz. pineapple juice

½ oz. lime or lemon juice

Lime slice

Combine all ingredients except the lime slice in a shaker with cracked ice. Shake vigorously, then pour into the serving glass. Garnish with lime slice.

Tequila Sunrise
Serve in a chilled Collins glass.

1½ oz. white or gold tequila   ¾ oz. grenadine

Juice of ½ lime   Lime slice

3 oz. orange juice

Combine all ingredients except grenadine and lime slice in a shaker with cracked ice. Shake vigorously, then pour into the serving glass. *Carefully* add the grenadine. *Do not stir!* Garnish with lime slice.

Tequila Sunset
Serve in a chilled Collins glass.

1¹/₂ oz. white tequila   Orange juice to fill

3 dashes lime juice   ¹/₂ oz. blackberry brandy

Combine the tequila and lime juice in the serving glass filled with ice. Add orange juice to fill. Stir. *Carefully* pour the blackberry brandy into the drink down a twisted-handle bar spoon (see Chapter 2). Allow the brandy to rise from the bottom. *Do not stir!*

Citrus Mixers

Matador
Serve in a chilled cocktail glass.

1¹/₂ oz. white or gold tequila   1 oz. lime juice

3 oz. pineapple juice   ¹/₂ tsp. sugar syrup

Combine all ingredients in a shaker with ice. Shake vigorously, then strain into the serving glass.

Changuirongo
Serve on the rocks in a Collins glass.

1¹/₂ oz. white or gold tequila

Citrus-flavored soda

Lime or lemon wedge

Combine tequila and soda over ice in the serving glass. Garnish with the fruit wedge.

Tequila with Liqueur

Brave Bull
Serve in a chilled old-fashioned glass.

1½ oz. white tequila   Lemon twist

¾ oz. Kahlúa

Combine all ingredients except the twist in a shaker with cracked ice. Shake vigorously, then pour into the glass. Garnish with the twist.

Crazy Nun
Serve in an old-fashioned glass filled with finely crushed ice.

1½ oz. white or gold tequila

1½ oz. anisette

Combine all ingredients in the serving glass filled with finely crushed ice. Stir well.

Tequila with Rum—Yes, Rum

Berta's Special
Serve in a chilled tall Collins glass.

2 oz. tequila   1 egg white

Juice of 1 lime   Club soda to fill

1 tsp. sugar syrup   Lime juice
(may substitute honey)

Liberal dashes orange bitters

Combine all ingredients except the club soda in a shaker with cracked ice. Shake vigorously, then pour into the serving glass. Add club soda to fill. Garnish with the lime slice.

Quick One

Man at the bar is coughing and sneezing over his tequila-and-orange juice.

"Sick?" asks the fellow on the next stool.

"Doc told me that the only way to kill these kind of germs is plenty of orange juice."

"Oh, I see."

"Trouble is: How do I get *them* to drink it?"

Coco Loco

Serve in a coconut (see directions).

1 coconut	1 oz. pineapple juice
1 oz. white tequila	Sugar syrup to taste
1 oz. gin	$^1/_2$ fresh lime
1 oz. light rum	

Prepare the coconut by carefully sawing off the top. Do not spill out the coconut milk. Add cracked ice to the coconut, then pour in the liquid ingredients. Squeeze in the lime juice, then drop in the lime shell. Stir. Sip through straws.

Bar Tips

You'll find a recipe for a tequila martini—the Tequini—in Chapter 5.

As popular as it has become in the United States, tequila is still *relatively* new to American drinkers, and there is a great deal of room for new tequila inventions. In the meantime, bold bartenders and drinkers have found places for tequila in a host of trusted standbys. For example, the sour turns out to be a natural with tequila. Don't use sour mix, but lime or lemon juice instead. The Tequila Manhattan requires a premium-label *tequila añejo*. Go easy on the sweet vermouth. See Appendix B for a full list of classic tequila variations.

Chapter 12

Brandies and Liqueurs

In This Chapter
➤ V.S.O.P. and other coded messages
➤ How brandy and liqueurs are made
➤ Brandy vs. cognac
➤ "Flavored" or "fruit" brandies and cognac recipes
➤ Liqueur recipes

Today, brandy—and especially its regal incarnation as cognac—is regarded with feelings ranging from respect to awe, and, like fine champagne, it has earned a place of honor as a ceremonial libation, typically reserved for special occasions. That's fine, but brandy also makes a delicious and very useful mixer in a host of drinks that you can enjoy any time.

That's VSOP, Not RSVP

Part of the brandy/cognac mystique is locked within the letters *V.O.* or *V.S.O.P.* printed on the label. You need be puzzled no longer. V.O. just stands for *very old*, but is, in fact, applied to brandies of a rather young age (as brandy goes), at least four and a half years. V.S.O.P. stands for *very superior old pale* and indicates a truly old brandy, usually 10 years old or more.

Bar Tips

Unlike wine, brandy stops aging once it is removed from the wooden cask and bottled, so the bottling date is of no significance. There is a practical limit to how long brandy may age. After about 60 years, aging becomes deterioration.

What does aging do to brandy? The effect is twofold. To begin with, there is simply something magical about consuming a drink that was prepared years ago. You're dipping, quite literally, into history. More directly, however, aging renders the flavor of brandy or cognac more complex, more subtle, more interesting, and makes the drink smoother and mellower.

Cognac—The Regal

Everything about cognac takes time and care. Not only are the grapes carefully cultivated and selected, but distillation is carried out in *alembics*, which are ancient devices that turn out distillate one batch at a time (in contrast to modern continuous stills, which are suited to mass production). Less expensive brandies are distilled in continuous stills rather than in the much more demanding alembics.

Buzzed Words

Champagne, as applied to cognac, has nothing to do with the sparkling wine. The word is French for flat, open country, and its English equivalent is *plain*.

Flavored Brandies

Calvados is an example of a *flavored brandy*—that is, a brandy based on a fruit other than the grape. The French—as well as distillers in other countries—offer a wide range of flavored or "fruit" brandies, including pear brandy (which typically comes bottled with an entire Bartlett pear inside), raspberry brandy (known as *framboise*), strawberry brandy (*fraise*), plum brandy (*mirabelle*), and cherry brandy (*kirsch*). Burgundy's *marc* is made from the *pomace* (skin and pulp) of grapes, rather than the grape juice. The result is a most aggressive and flavorful brandy.

The Alexanders

Brandy Alexander

Serve in a chilled cocktail glass.

1¹⁄₂ oz. brandy

1 oz. crème de cacao

1 oz. heavy cream

Combine all ingredients in a shaker with ice. Shake vigorously, then strain into the serving glass.

Alexander's Sister de Menthe
Serve in a chilled cocktail glass.

1½ oz. brandy

1 oz. white crème de menthe

1 oz. heavy cream

Combine all ingredients in a shaker with ice. Shake vigorously, then strain into the serving glass.

Alexander's Sister Kahlúa
Serve in a chilled cocktail glass.

1½ oz. brandy

1 oz. Kahlúa

1 oz. heavy cream

Combine all ingredients in a shaker with ice. Shake vigorously, then strain into the serving glass.

Other Brandy Classics

Brandy and Soda
Serve on the rocks in a lowball glass.

1½ oz. brandy

4 or 5 oz. club soda

Combine the ingredients over ice in the serving glass.

Brandy Flip
Serve in a chilled wine glass.

2 oz. brandy $1/2$ oz. cream (optional)

1 egg   Ground nutmeg

1 tsp. sugar syrup

Combine all ingredients except nutmeg in a blender with cracked ice. Blend until smooth, then pour into the serving glass. Sprinkle with nutmeg.

Sidecar
Serve in a chilled cocktail glass.

$1^1/2$ oz. brandy $1/2$ oz. lemon juice

$3/4$ oz. curaçao

Combine all ingredients in a shaker with ice. Shake vigorously, then strain into the serving glass.

Stinger
Serve in a chilled cocktail glass.

$1^1/2$ oz. brandy

$1^1/2$ oz. white crème de menthe

Combine all ingredients in a shaker with ice. Shake vigorously, then strain into the serving glass.

Apple Blossom with Juice
Serve in a chilled cocktail glass.

$1^1/2$ oz. brandy   1 tsp. lemon juice

1 oz. apple juice   Lemon slice

Combine all ingredients except the lemon slice in a shaker with ice. Shake vigorously, then strain into the serving glass. Garnish with the lemon slice.

Apricot Excursions

Apricot Brandy Fizz
Serve in a chilled old-fashioned glass.

2 oz. apricot brandy

Liberal dash or two grenadine

Orange slice

Lemon twist

Club soda to fill

Combine brandy and grenadine in the serving glass one third filled with ice. Garnish with orange slice and lemon twist, then add club soda to fill.

Toast
May you never lie, cheat, or drink—but if you must lie, lie in one another's arms, and if you must cheat, cheat death, and if you must drink, drink with all of us.

Apricot Brandy Sour
Serve in a chilled cocktail glass.

2 oz. apricot brandy

1 oz. lemon juice

1 tsp. sugar syrup

Lemon slice

Combine all ingredients except the lemon slice in a shaker with ice. Shake vigorously, then strain into the serving glass. Garnish with the lemon slice.

Cherry Mixtures

Cherry Blossom
Serve in a chilled cocktail glass.

1$^1/_2$ oz. brandy

$^3/_4$ oz. cherry brandy (may substitute cherry liqueur)

$^1/_2$ oz. curaçao

$^1/_2$ oz. lemon juice

$^1/_4$ oz. grenadine

1 tsp. sugar syrup

Combine all ingredients in a shaker with cracked ice. Shake vigorously, then strain into the serving glass. If you wish, rim the glass with brandy and powdered sugar.

Cherry Hill
Serve in a chilled cocktail glass.

1 oz. brandy

1 oz. cherry brandy (may substitute cherry liqueur)

$^1/_2$ oz. dry vermouth

Orange twist

Combine all ingredients except orange twist in a shaker with cracked ice. Shake vigorously, then pour into the serving glass. Garnish with orange twist.

Peachy Potables

Peach Fizz
Serve in a chilled Collins glass.

1¹/₂ oz. brandy	1 tsp. sugar syrup
1¹/₂ oz. peach brandy	Club soda to fill
¹/₂ oz. lemon juice	Fresh or brandied peach slice
1 tsp. crème de banana	

Combine all ingredients except soda and peach slice in a shaker with cracked ice. Shake vigorously, then pour into the serving glass. Add club soda to fill and garnish with the peach slice.

Peachtree Sling
Serve in a chilled Collins glass.

1¹/₂ oz. brandy	Club soda to fill
1¹/₂ oz. peach brandy	Brandied or fresh peach slice
¹/₂ oz. lemon juice	1 tsp. peach liqueur
¹/₂ oz. sugar syrup	

Combine all ingredients except soda, peach slice, and peach liqueur in a shaker with cracked ice. Shake vigorously, then pour into the serving glass. Add club soda to fill, then garnish with the peach slice. Spoon on the peach liqueur as a float. Do not stir.

B&B Variations

B&B is a classic combination of Benedictine and brandy—preferably premium-label cognac. It is a delicious after-dinner drink.

Another B&B favorite is the B&B Collins. Brandy works well here, but, for a special treat, use cognac.

B&B
Serve in a snifter.

1 oz. cognac

1 oz. Benedictine

Combine all ingredients in snifter and swirl.

B&B Collins
Serve in a chilled Collins glass.

2 oz. cognac	Club soda to fill
1–2 oz. lemon juice	1/2 oz. Benedictine
1 tsp. sugar syrup	Lemon slice

Combine all ingredients except soda, Benedictine, and lemon slice in a shaker with cracked ice. Shake vigorously, then pour into the serving glass. Add club soda to fill. Carefully pour on the Benedictine as a float. Do not stir. Garnish with the lemon slice.

Brandy and Champagne

Brandy and champagne make a sophisticated combination.

Champagne Cooler
Serve in a chilled wine goblet.

1 oz. brandy	Champagne to fill
1 oz. Cointreau	Mint sprig

Combine brandy and Cointreau in the serving glass. Add champagne to fill and stir very gently. Garnish with mint sprig.

Chicago

Serve in a chilled wine goblet rimmed with sugar.

Lemon wedge	Dash curaçao
Superfine sugar	Dash Angostura bitters
1¹/₂ oz. brandy	Champagne to fill

Run the lemon wedge around the serving glass rim to moisten. Roll the moistened rim in sugar to coat. Combine brandy, curaçao, and bitters in a mixing glass with ice. Stir well, then strain into the serving glass. Add champagne to fill.

King's Peg

Serve in a chilled wine goblet.

3 oz. cognac

Brut champagne to fill

Pour cognac into the serving glass, then add champagne to fill.

Liqueurs—also called cordials—occupy a realm between the manufacture of spirits and the esoteric lore of alchemy. Ounce for ounce, you won't find stronger, more compelling, or more varied flavors than those distilled into liqueur. No distilled spirit has a more varied, more venerable, or more interesting past than the liqueurs, which partake both of ancient tradition and modern top-secret technology.

Bar Tips

If you or a guest spill a sticky, colored liqueur on a fancy suit or dress, immediately soak the stain with club soda. Follow with plain water, and rub a bit of Ivory bar soap directly on the stain. Rinse with cold water, then blot dry.

Liqueur with Liquor

Combinations of liqueur with hard liquor are deceptively potent. The liqueur makes the liquor go down easy and, before you know it, you're buzzed. Enjoy—but pace yourself by drinking responsibly.

Barracuda

Serve in a carved-out pineapple shell.

$^1/_2$ oz. Galliano	Champagne to fill
1 oz. gold rum	Lime slice
1 oz. pineapple juice	Maraschino cherry
$^1/_4$ oz. lime juice	Pineapple shell
$^1/_4$ oz. sugar syrup	

Combine all ingredients except champagne, lime slice, and cherry in a shaker with cracked ice. Shake vigorously, then pour into the pineapple shell. Add champagne to fill. Garnish with the lime slice and the cherry.

Café Kahlúa
Serve in a chilled old-fashioned glass.

3 oz. Kahlúa	2 oz. cream
1½ oz. gold Jamaica rum	Cinnamon stick

Combine all ingredients except cinnamon stick in a shaker with cracked ice. Shake vigorously, then pour into the serving glass. Garnish with the cinnamon stick.

Bar Tips
Serve drinks containing dairy products fresh, just as you would serve milk alone.

Grand Hotel
Serve in a chilled cocktail glass.

1½ oz. Grand Marnier	Dash lemon juice
1½ oz. gin	Lemon twist
½ oz. dry vermouth	

Combine all ingredients except the twist in a shaker with cracked ice. Shake vigorously, then pour into the serving glass. Garnish with the twist.

Mazatlán
Serve in a chilled cocktail glass.

1 oz. white crème de cacao $^1/_2$ oz. coconut cream

1 oz. light rum   1 oz. cream

Combine all ingredients in a shaker with ice. Shake vigorously, then strain into the serving glass.

Melon Ball
Serve on the rocks in a highball glass.

1 oz. vodka

$^1/_2$ oz. Midori melon liqueur

5 oz. orange juice

Combine the vodka and Midori in the serving glass filled with ice. Add orange juice and stir well.

Melon Patch
Serve in a chilled highball glass.

1 oz. Midori melon liqueur   Club soda to fill

$^1/_2$ oz. triple sec   Orange slice

$^1/_2$ oz. vodka

Combine all ingredients except club soda and orange slice in the serving glass one third full of ice. Stir well, then add club soda to fill and garnish with the orange slice.

Cordial Favorites

Alabama Slammer Highball
Serve in a highball glass.

$^1/_2$ oz. sloe gin	3 oz. orange juice
$^1/_2$ oz. Southern Comfort	Maraschino cherry
$^1/_2$ oz. triple sec	Orange slice
$^1/_2$ oz. Galliano	

Combine all ingredients except fruit in a shaker filled with ice. Shake vigorously, then strain into the serving glass. Add more ice, if you wish. Garnish with the cherry and orange slice.

Alabama Slammer Shooter
Serve in shot glasses.

$1^1/_2$ oz. sloe gin	$1^1/_2$ oz. Southern Comfort
$1^1/_2$ oz. amaretto	$1^1/_2$ oz. orange juice

Combine all ingredients in a shaker with ice. Shake vigorously, then strain into shot glasses. Yields four shots.

Sloe Gin Fizz
Serve in a chilled Collins glass.

1 oz. sloe gin	Club soda to fill
2 oz. sour mix	Maraschino cherry

Combine the sloe gin and sour mix in a shaker filled with ice. Shake vigorously, then strain into the serving glass. Add club soda to fill, then garnish with the cherry.

Grasshopper
Serve in a chilled cocktail glass.

1 oz. green crème de menthe

1 oz. white crème de cacao

1 oz. light cream

Combine all ingredients in a blender with ice.
Shake vigorously, then strain into the serving glass.

Pink Squirrel
Serve in chilled cocktail glass.

1 oz. crème de noyaux

1 oz. white crème de cacao

1 oz. cream

Combine all ingredients in a shaker with ice. Shake
vigorously, then strain into the serving glass.

Chapter 13

Up in Flames: Hot and Flaming Drinks

In This Chapter

➤ Attractions of hot drinks

➤ Fortified coffee drinks

➤ How to flame drinks dramatically and safely

➤ Hot drink recipes

The human body is a furnace. Heat is precious to it, and what is precious feels good. That, in essence, is the attraction of hot drinks, whether it's tea, coffee, or hot chocolate. Add alcohol to a hot drink, and that thermal glow spreads, mellows, and is sustained. In the days before central heating, no self-respecting inn would fail, in wintertime, to offer toddies or mulled drinks. The flip, an American colonial favorite consisting of spirits, ale, eggs, sugar, cream, and assorted spices, was heated on demand with a "flip iron"—a poker kept hot on the fireplace grate for the purpose of heating and frothing drinks.

Fortified Coffees of All Nations

The most obvious hot drink vehicle is America's favorite hot beverage: coffee. The most popular fortified coffees have international themes, derived from the kind of spirit used to fuel them.

Amaretto Café (Italian Coffee)
Serve in a coffee mug.

1¹/₂ oz. amaretto

Hot coffee to fill

Whipped cream

Pour the amaretto into the mug and add hot coffee to fill. Top with whipped cream.

Bar Tips
When mixing spirits with coffee, pour the spirit in first. Then add the coffee.

Roman Coffee
Serve in a coffee mug.

1¹/₂ oz. Galliano

Coffee to fill

Whipped cream

Pour Galliano into the mug. Add coffee to fill and top with whipped cream.

Café Mexicano
Serve in a coffee mug.

1 oz. Kahlúa

$1/2$ oz. white or gold tequila

Hot coffee

Whipped cream (optional)

Pour the Kahlúa and tequila in the mug. Add coffee. Top with whipped cream, if you wish.

Café Bonaparte
Serve in a coffee mug or hot drink glass.

$1^1/2$ oz. brandy

Cappuccino to fill

Pour the brandy into the serving glass, then fill with cappuccino.

Café Marnier
Serve in a coffee mug.

$1^1/2$ oz. Grand Marnier

Espresso to fill

Whipped cream (optional)

Pour the Grand Marnier into the mug. Add espresso to three-fourths full. Stir and add whipped cream, if you wish.

Irish Coffee
Serve in a coffee mug.

1½ oz. Irish whiskey   Coffee

1 tsp. sugar   Whipped cream

Pour whiskey into the mug. Add sugar. Add coffee to fill and top with whipped cream.

Creamy Irish Coffee
Serve in a coffee mug.

1½ oz. Bailey's Irish Cream

Coffee to fill

Whipped cream

Pour the liqueur into the mug. Add coffee to fill and top with whipped cream.

Jamaican Coffee
Serve in a coffee mug.

1 oz. Tia Maria   Whipped cream

¾ oz. rum (white, gold, or dark)   Grated nutmeg

Coffee to fill

Pour Tia Maria and rum into the mug. Add coffee to fill, top with whipped cream, and sprinkle with nutmeg.

Café Zurich
Serve in a coffee mug.

1^1/$_2$ oz. anisette	Coffee
1^1/$_2$ oz. cognac	1 tsp. honey
^{1}/$_2$ oz. amaretto	Whipped cream

Pour the spirits into the coffee mug. Add hot coffee to three-fourths full. Float a teaspoon of honey on top of the drink, then top the honey with whipped cream.

Comfort Mocha
Serve in a mug.

1^1/$_2$ oz. Southern Comfort	Boiling water to fill
1 tsp. instant cocoa	Whipped cream
1 tsp. instant coffee	

Combine all ingredients except the whipped cream in a mug with boiling water. Top with whipped cream.

Hot Rum Drinks

Hot Grog
Serve in a mug.

1 tsp. sugar	Juice of ^{1}/$_4$ lemon
1^1/$_2$ oz. rum	Boiling water to three-fourths full

Place sugar in the mug, then add rum and the lemon juice. Finally, add boiling water to three-fourths full. Stir.

Hot Buttered Rum
Serve in a mug.

1 tsp. sugar	2 oz. white, gold, or dark rum
1 tsp. butter	Boiling water to three-fourths full

Put the sugar and butter in the mug, then add the rum. Pour in boiling water to three-fourths full. Stir.

Buzzed Words

A **hot toddy** is any alcohol-based sweetened hot drink. It may be shortened simply to **toddy**. There is no such thing as a cold toddy.

Toddy Collection

Your Basic Hot Toddy
Serve in a mug.

1 tsp. sugar

2 oz. blended whiskey

Boiling water to three-fourths full

Put the sugar in the mug, then add the whiskey. Add boiling water to three-fourths full. Stir.

Hot Toddy with Bourbon
Serve in a mug.

1 tsp. sugar	4 oz. boiling water
3 whole cloves	1 oz. bourbon
Cinnamon stick	Grated nutmeg
Lemon slice	

Put the sugar, cloves, cinnamon stick, and lemon slice into the mug. Add 1 oz. of the boiling water and stir. After letting the mixture steep for five minutes, pour in the bourbon and the rest of the boiling water. Stir. Dust with nutmeg.

You may vary either of these toddies by using brandy, rum, gin, or vodka instead of blended whiskey or bourbon.

Comfort Drinks

Just about any hot drink you can make is soothing, but the following recipes will summon up visions of true nirvana.

Bar Tips

Wine and most liqueurs cannot endure boiling. The flavor as well as much of the alcoholic content will go up in steam.

Mulled Claret
Serve in a mug.

5 oz. red Bordeaux	Pinch grated nutmeg
1 oz. port	A few whole cloves
$^3/_4$ oz. brandy	Lemon twist
Pinch ground cinnamon	

Combine all ingredients in a saucepan and heat, but do not boil. Pour into the mug.

Mulled Claret Batch
Yield: 13 drinks

2 oz. honey	6 whole cloves
1 750 ml. bottle red Bordeaux	Few cinnamon sticks, broken
1 pt. ruby port	$^1/_2$ tsp. grated nutmeg
1 cup brandy	Lemon twist

In the flaming pan of a chafing dish over direct heat, dissolve the honey with 1 cup water. Add the Bordeaux, port, brandy, spices, and lemon. Heat over a low flame, stirring occasionally. Do not allow to boil.

Simple Mulled Cider
Serve in mugs.

3 oz. sugar	1 cinnamon stick per mug
3 pints hard cider	Pinch allspice per mug
4 oz. rum	

Combine ingredients in a pot. Heat and stir, but do not boil. Strain into the mug. The recipe yields three large or five smaller drinks.

Buzzed Words

Hard cider is fermented cider and, therefore, alcoholic. **Sweet cider** is nonalcoholic apple cider.

Going to Blazes

Few acts of mixology are more impressive than setting a drink ablaze. The effect is not only theatrical; done correctly, it enhances the flavor of the drink and, most importantly, results in no injury to oneself or one's guests.

Bar Tips

A flaming drink is *not* to be consumed while it is flaming. This may sound like superfluous advice. Who'd be dumb enough to drink fire? But in some college bars and elsewhere, the idea is to down a flaming drink at once, so that the alcohol vapor burns off above the glass, while the liquor is safely downed. Raising a flaming drink to your face, then trying to drink it, is always a very bad idea.

Don't Try This at Home!

Most liquor has a relatively low concentration of alcohol. If what you're working with is 80 proof, the liquid is only 40 percent alcohol. This means that it probably won't burn unless it is vaporized; therefore, your first step is to heat a *small* amount of alcohol before igniting it.

This said, it must be observed that *vaporized* alcohol, even at relatively low concentrations, is *very* flammable. So, before we get into the details of how to flame drinks, let's take time for a safety check:

➤ Use the smallest amount of liquor possible to flame drinks. For a single drink, an ounce is sufficient.

➤ Do not flame drinks near draperies, curtains, paper banners, bunting, streamers, or other combustible materials.

➤ Never heat or flame spirits in a chafing dish at the serving table. If the hot or flaming liquid should spill, you could end up burning a number of people. Instead, heating and flaming should be done on a stable cart or serving table apart from guests.

➤ Do not keep uncorked spirits near an open flame.

➤ Never add spirits into a flaming dish! There is a good chance that the vapors will ignite and the fire will blow back on you or someone else.

➤ Alcohol burns with a pale flame. If the lights in the room are bright, you and your guests may not see the flame. This is not only dangerous, but insufficiently spectacular. Dim the room lights before flaming.

➤ Generally, alcohol burns off quickly; however, always have a sufficiently large lid on hand to cover the chafing dish in order to put out a fire gone awry.

Bar Tips

The flaming drink is definitely not child's play. *Flaming alcohol is intensely hot and can cause serious burn injuries!* In addition to safety, it is important to flame drinks properly in order to preserve as well as enhance their flavor.

Ignition...Lift Off!

To flame a drink successfully and safely, begin by taking a single teaspoonful of the liquor you want to flame. Warm this over a lighted match in order to vaporize some of the alcohol. Ignite the liquor in the spoon, then carefully pour the flaming alcohol over the prepared recipe. Do *not* put your face near the drink you are flaming. Stand back.

Buzzed Words

As a verb, **flambé** means to drench with liquor and ignite. The word may also be used as a noun, synonymous with flaming drink.

Flaming Rum

Rum is well suited to the *flambé* because the flaming process creates a delicious collection of concentrated natural flavors.

Burning Blue Mountain

Serve in a egg nog–style mug.

5 oz. dark Jamaican rum	Lime rind, cut up
2 tsp. powdered sugar	Lemon twist
Orange rind, cut up	

Pour rum into a chafing dish and warm. Add sugar and fruit rinds. Stir to dissolve sugar, then ignite. Ladle the drink into the serving glass and garnish with the lemon twist.

Christmas Rum Punch
Serve in a punch bowl.

6 oranges	$^1/_2$ gallon sweet cider
Cloves	Powdered cinnamon
1 bottle dark rum	Grated nutmeg
Sugar to taste	

Prepare the oranges by sticking them with cloves, then baking until the oranges begin to brown. Slice the oranges and place in a punch bowl. Add rum. Add sugar to taste. Carefully ignite and allow to burn for a few minutes before extinguishing with the cider. Garnish with cinnamon and nutmeg.

Flaming Brandy

Brandy is the most frequently used fuel for flamed drinks.

Big Apple
Serve in a warmed 10-oz. mug.

3 oz. apple juice	3 tbs. baked apple
Pinch ground ginger	1 oz. apple brandy

Combine the apple juice and ginger in a saucepan. Heat and let simmer for a few minutes. Put the baked apple in the serving mug. Pour the apple brandy into a ladle. Warm the ladle over a match or a low gas flame. Ignite the brandy in the ladle, then pour over the baked apple. Extinguish the fire with the warm ginger-spiced apple juice. Stir. Serve warm, with a spoon for eating the apple.

Coffee Blazer

Serve in an old-fashioned glass.

1 tbs. Kahlúa	Lemon slice
1 tbs. cognac	Hot coffee to fill
Sugar	Whipped cream

Warm the Kahlúa and cognac over a match or low gas flame. Moisten the rim of the serving glass with the lemon slice, then roll the rim in sugar; drop the lemon slice in the glass. Warm the glass over a low flame to melt the sugar on the rim. Pour in the warmed Kahlúa and cognac and ignite. Extinguish with the coffee. Stir well and top with whipped cream.

Buzzed Word Glossary

absinthe   An aromatic, bitter, very strong (containing 68 percent alcohol) liqueur flavored chiefly with wormwood (*Artemisia absinthium*) and containing other botanicals— licorice, hyssop, fennel, angelica root, aniseed, and star aniseed. Famed as the favorite drink of Henri de Toulouse-Lautrec, absinthe was outlawed in many countries early in the 20th century because of its apparent toxicity.

aging   The storage of the distilled alcohol in wooden casks, most often oak. Over months or years, the wood reacts with the alcohol, imparting to it a distinctive color, aroma, and flavor.

alcoholism   The medical definition and the criteria of diagnosis of this condition vary, but, in general, this complex, chronic psychological and nutritional disorder may be defined as continued excessive or compulsive use of alcoholic drinks.

apéritif   A spiritous beverage taken before a meal as an appetizer. Its origin, in French, is hardly appetizing, however, originally denoting a purgative.

aquavit   Aqua vitae is not to be confused with *aquavit*, which is a very strong Scandinavian liquor distilled from potatoes and grain and flavored with caraway seeds.

arrack   A strong alcoholic beverage distilled from palm sap, rice, or molasses. It is popular in the Middle and Far East and is available in larger liquor stores.

barback An assistant or apprentice bartender, who does the bartender's scut work, including tapping beer kegs, running ice, replacing glassware, preparing and stocking garnishes, restocking shelves, and so on.

blackout Not a loss of consciousness, but an inability to remember, even after you are sober, what you did and said while intoxicated.

blended whiskey A blended whiskey may be a combination of *straight* whiskeys and neutral, flavorless whiskeys (this is true of Canadian whisky) or it may be a combination of similar whiskey products made by different distillers at different times (as in blended scotch).

blood-alcohol concentration (BAC) The concentration of alcohol in the blood, expressed as the weight of alcohol in a fixed volume of blood. Sometimes called *blood alcohol level* or BAL. It is used as an objective measure of intoxication.

bottled-in-bond Whiskey that, by federal law, must be a 100-proof, straight whiskey aged at least four years and stored in a federally bonded warehouse pending sale. Not until the whiskey is sold—withdrawn from the bonded warehouse—does the distiller have to pay the federal excise tax. Beyond these requirements, the "bottled-in-bond" designation says nothing about the quality or nature of the whiskey.

branch water Water withdrawn from the local "branch," or stream. Sadly, in most U.S. locations, this would be a risky undertaking these days, and "branch" or "branch water" is just a romantic appellation to describe what comes out of the faucet.

champagne As applied to cognac, champagne has nothing to do with the sparkling wine. The word is French for flat, open country, and its English-language equivalent is *plain*.

cobbler Traditionally, an iced drink made of wine or liqueur plus sugar and fruit juice.

Coffey still See *continuous still*.

congeners Acids, aldehydes, esters, ketones, phenols, and tannins that are byproducts of fermentation, distillation, and aging. These "impurities" may contribute to the character and flavor of the spirit, but they cause undesirable effects in some people, notably increasing the intensity of hangover.

continuous still Also called a Coffey still, after the inventor, Aeneas Coffey. A type of still for whiskey distillation that allows for continuous high-volume production, as opposed to the *pot still*, which must be emptied and "recharged" one batch at a time.

cordial In modern usage, a synonym for *liqueur*; however, the word originally designated only those liqueurs thought to have tonic or medicinal efficacy.

daiquiri A rum, lime juice, sugar drink named after the Cuban town near the original Bacardi rum distillery.

daisy A whiskey- or gin-based drink that includes some sweet syrup and a float of—usually golden—liqueur.

distilling The process of evaporating the alcohol produced by fermentation, then condensing the evaporated fluid to concentrate and purify it. The increase in alcohol concentration is usually great.

dry martini A martini with relatively little vermouth versus gin. Some drinkers prefer 12 parts gin to 1 part vermouth, while others insist on a 20-to-1 ratio. Extremists do away with the vermouth altogether and have a gin and olive on the rocks.

dry gin You will often encounter the expression *dry gin* or *London dry gin* on bottle labels. These designations originated when gin was widely available in "sweet" (called *Old Tom*) as well as "dry" forms. Today, the distinction is mainly superfluous, because almost all English and American gin is now dry. Also note that a gin does not have to be made in London or even in England to bear the "London dry gin" designation on its label. This describes a manufacturing style, not a place of origin.

DUI or DWI   In some jurisdictions, drunk driving is called driving under the influence—*DUI*—in others, it's driving while intoxicated—*DWI*.

ethyl alcohol   The potable alcohol obtained from the fermentation of sugars and starches. For producing hard liquor, the ethyl alcohol is purified and concentrated by distillation.

fermenting   The chemical process whereby complex organic substances are split into relatively simple compounds. In the manufacture of alcohol, special yeasts are used to ferment—convert—the starches and sugars of grain (or some other organic substance) into alcohol.

fizz   Any drink made with soda and a sweetener.

flambé   As a verb, *flambé* means to drench with liquor and ignite. The word may also be used as a noun, synonymous with flaming drink.

flip   A drink containing liquor, sugar, spice, and egg. Often served hot. Flips were most popular in the 18th and 19th centuries.

fortified wine   A fermented wine to which a distilled spirit, usually brandy, has been added. Brandy itself is often considered a fortified wine.

freeze   A frozen drink.

garbage   A bit of fruit or vegetable added to a drink primarily for the sake of appearance. It does not significantly enhance the flavor of the drink.

garnish   A bit of fruit or vegetable added to a drink principally to enhance its flavor.

generic liqueurs   Liqueurs prepared according to standard formulas by a number of distillers.

grog   Originally, grog was nothing more than rum diluted with water and rationed to sailors of the 18th-century Royal Navy. Its namesake was Admiral Edward Vernon (1684–1757), who first ordered the ration: Vernon's nickname was

Old Grogram, after his habit of wearing a grogram (coarse wool) cloak.

hard liquor   A beverage with a high alcoholic content. Gin, vodka, bourbon, sour mash whiskey, scotch, blended whiskey, rye, rum, and tequila are the most common "hard liquors."

hard cider   Fermented—and therefore alcoholic—apple cider.

jigger   The glass or the metal measuring cup used to measure drinks. It is also what you call the amount the jigger measures: $1^1/_2$ ounces.

light whiskey   Whiskey distilled at a high proof (in excess of 160 proof) and aged in used charred oak barrels. Light whiskey is more flavorful than neutral spirits, but not as strongly flavored as straight whiskey. It is an important component in blended whiskey.

liquor   Any alcoholic beverage made by fermentation *and* distillation rather than fermentation alone (as is the case with wine and beer).

London dry gin   See *dry gin.*

macerate   To make soft by soaking in liquid. Applied to the production of liqueurs, maceration is a process of soaking botanicals in the distilled alcohol to extract their flavor.

malt   Grain (usually barley) that has been allowed to sprout. Used as material for fermentation to produce beer or certain distilled spirits.

malting   The practice of allowing the grain (usually barley) to sprout before fermentation. In whiskey production, this produces a variety of characteristic flavors in the finished product.

mash   The fermentable starchy mixture from which an alcoholic beverage is produced.

master blender The craftsperson in charge of selecting and proportioning the component whiskies that make up a blended whiskey.

mixed-grain whiskey Whiskey distilled from a mash in which no single type of grain predominates. Contrast straight whiskey, which is made from mash containing at least 51 percent of a certain grain.

muddle To mash and stir. One muddles such things as mint leaves and other solids in order to make a suspension or a paste with fluid. A special pestle-like wooden *muddler* can be used, but any spoon will do.

muddler See *muddle*.

mull To heat and spice a drink. Traditionally, the heating was done by inserting a hot poker into the drink; today, *mulled* drinks are usually heated on a stove.

Old Tom A special form of gin, slightly sweetened. It is not widely enjoyed today and may be quite hard to find.

pony Strictly speaking, a 1-ounce measure; however, pony glasses range in capacity from 1 to 2 ounces.

port (also called *porto*) Named after the Portuguese town of Oporto, birthplace of this fortified wine and the origin of "true" port today—though other regions also produce port wines. Port is sweet, whereas sherry ranges from dry to sweet.

posset A traditional English drink made with sweetened milk that has been curdled by the addition of wine or ale. It is usually served hot.

pot still See *continuous still*.

pousse-café A drink made with two or more liqueurs and, sometimes, cream. The different spirits vary in specific gravity, so float in discrete layers if carefully combined. The layered effect is novel and pretty.

proof The alcoholic content of a spirit. It is determined by multiplying the percentage of alcoholic content by two, so that liquor that is 40 percent alcohol is 80 proof.

proprietary liqueurs "Brand-name" products prepared according to closely guarded trade-secret formulas that are the property of specific distillers.

rickey Any alcohol-based drink with soda water and lime—and sometimes sugar.

sangria A cold drink made with red (sometimes white) wine mixed with brandy, sugar, fruit juice, and soda. Its blood-red color and red-blooded robustness are underscored by the meaning of the word in Spanish: the act of bleeding.

schnapps A word used to describe any number of strong, dry liquors, but, recently, has been applied to a variety of flavored liqueurs. The word derives from the German original, spelled with one *p* and meaning "mouthful."

scut work The menial chores behind the bar, such as tapping beer kegs, running ice, stocking shelves, and so on; often performed by a *barback*.

sherry A fortified Spanish wine with a nutlike flavor. Its name is an Anglicization of Jerez, a city in southwestern Spain, where sherry was first produced and from which region the most highly respected sherry still comes.

shooter A drink meant to be downed in a single shot, often accompanied by table banging and gasps of pleasurable pain.

sling Any brandy, whiskey, or gin drink that is sweetened and flavored with lemon.

sloe gin Despite the name, *sloe gin* is not a gin at all, but a sweet liqueur. Its principal flavoring is the sloe berry, the small, sour fruit of the blackthorn.

specific gravity Applied to liquids, *specific gravity* is the ratio of the mass of the liquid to the mass of an equal volume of distilled water at 39 degrees Fahrenheit.

spirits (or *spirit*) A generic term for an alcoholic beverage based on distilled *liquor*.

spritzer   A combination of wine—usually Rhine wine or other white wine—and club soda or seltzer. The word comes from the German for *spray*.

still   A device for distilling liquids (including alcohol) to concentrate and purify them. In its simplest form, it consists of a vessel in which the liquid is heated to vapor, a coil (or other apparatus) to cool and condense the vapor, and a vessel to collect the condensed vapor (called the distillate). Stills are made in a great many varieties, ranging from small batch stills to huge industrial continuous stills, capable of producing large volumes of distillate.

straight whiskey   The term *straight whiskey* is not to be confused with ordering "whiskey, straight" (that is, "neat," with neither ice, water, nor a mixer). The mash for straight whiskey contains at least 51 percent of a certain grain: straight malt whiskey mash contains 51 percent barley; straight rye, 51 percent rye; and straight bourbon, 51 percent corn; however, straight corn whiskey is made from mash that contains 80 percent corn.

surface tension   A molecular property of liquids by which the surface of the liquid tends to contract, taking on the characteristics of a stretched elastic membrane.

sweet cider   Nonalcoholic apple cider.

tequila añejo Tequila that has been aged in oak casks. It acquires a deep gold coloring and is therefore often called gold tequila; however, not all gold tequila is aged. Unaged tequila is clear and called *white* tequila.

toddy   A hot drink consisting of liquor—often rum—water, sugar, and spices.

whiskey versus whisky   American and Irish distillers spell the word with an *e*, while Scotch and Canadian distillers jump right from the *k* to the *y*.

wort   A soluble starch in the form of an infusion of malt. It is used in the fermentation processes of making whiskey and beer.

Last Call

The recipes presented in the main body of this book are all tried and all true. For the more adventurous bartender and drinker, however, we have collected some very intriguing new or out-of-the-ordinary drinks.

This is the place to come when you're stumped behind the bar, or just looking for something unusual to knock the socks off your guests. You've become familiar with most of the recipes commonly associated with each spirit. Now explore some variations on the original recipe—or stroll down entirely new avenues with intoxicating combinations like Between the Sheets, the Woo Woo, or the impressive Ramos Gin Fizz.

Walk on the Wild Side

Some of the following are new, some not so new, but all are—shall we say—highly stimulating. They are not for the scotch-and-water or Whiskey Sour crowd.

B-52

Serve straight-up in a shot glass.

$1/2$ oz. Grand Marnier

$1/2$ oz. Bailey's Irish Cream

$1/2$ oz. Kahlúa

Combine ingredients in a mixing glass, stir, then pour into the shot glass.

Bahama Mama

Serve in a chilled Collins glass.

Dash grenadine	1 oz. pineapple juice
$1^1/2$ oz. light rum	$2^1/2$ oz. orange juice
$1^1/2$ oz. gold rum	Maraschino cherry
$1^1/2$ oz. dark rum	Orange slice
2 oz. sour mix	

Put a dash of grenadine in the bottom of the serving glass and set aside. Combine all other ingredients except the cherry and orange slice in a shaker filled with ice. Shake vigorously, then pour into the ser-ving glass. Garnish with the cherry and orange slice.

Brain

Serve straight-up in a shot glass.

$3/4$ oz. Kahlúa

$3/4$ oz. vodka

Splash Bailey's Irish Cream

Combine the Kahlúa and vodka in the shot glass, then splash in the Bailey's. Do not stir. The swirling of the Bailey's creates the texture that suggests a brain.

Jell-O Shots

Serve solid and eat with a spoon,
or serve semigelatinous in shot glasses.

12 oz. vodka

6 oz. Jell-O gelatin mix (choose flavor)

12 oz. water

Combine 6 oz. vodka with 6 oz. water in a saucepan. Bring to a boil and stir in Jell-O gelatin mix. Remove from stove and add remaining 6 oz. of water and 6 oz. of vodka. Let set in the refrigerator overnight.

Note: Whether in fully gelled or in semiliquid/ semigelatinous form, this drink tends to retard the body's absorption of the alcohol, making it more difficult to tell when you have had "enough."

Kamikaze

Serve in a chilled cocktail glass.

1 oz. triple sec   1 oz. lime juice

1 oz. vodka

Combine all ingredients in a shaker with ice. Shake vigorously, then strain into the serving glass.

Long Island Iced Tea

Serve in a chilled Collins glass.

$^1/_2$ oz. gin   3 oz. sour mix

$^1/_2$ oz. vodka   Cola

$^1/_2$ oz. white tequila   Lemon wedge

$^1/_2$ oz. light rum   Mint sprigs

$^1/_2$ oz. white crème de menthe

Combine all ingredients except the cola, lemon wedge, and mint sprig with cracked ice in a blender. Blend well, then pour into the serving glass. Add cola to fill, and garnish with the lemon wedge and mint sprig.

Melon Ball Sunrise

Serve on the rocks in a highball glass.

1 oz. vodka   Orange juice to fill

1/2 oz. Midori melon liqueur   Drop grenadine

Combine vodka and Midori in the serving glass filled with ice. Add orange juice to fill. Stir well. Insert bar spoon into drink and slide a drop of grenadine down it. Allow the grenadine to rise from the bottom of the drink for the sunrise effect. Do not stir.

Midori Sour

Serve in a chilled whiskey sour glass.

2 oz. Midori

1 oz. lemon juice

1 tsp. sugar syrup

Combine all ingredients in a shaker with ice. Shake vigorously, then strain into the serving glass.

Sex on the Beach

Serve on the rocks in a highball glass.

1 1/2 oz. vodka

1 oz. peach schnapps

Cranberry juice to three-fourths full

Orange juice to fill

Combine all ingredients in the serving glass full of ice. Stir.

Toasted Almond

Serve in a chilled highball glass.

$1/2$ oz. Kahlúa

$1/2$ oz. amaretto

2 oz. cream

Combine all ingredients in a shaker filled with ice. Shake vigorously, then strain into the serving glass. Add more ice, if you wish.

Woo Woo

Serve on the rocks in a highball glass.

$3/4$ oz. vodka

$3/4$ oz. peach schnapps

3 oz. cranberry juice cocktail

Combine the ingredients over ice in the serving glass. Stir well.

More Joys of Gin

Dubonnet Cocktail

Serve straight-up or on the rocks in a chilled old-fashioned or lowball glass.

$1^1/2$ oz. gin

$1^1/2$ oz. Dubonnet rouge

Lemon twist

Vigorously shake the gin and Dubonnet, with ice, in a shaker or blend; pour into the serving glass. Garnish with a lemon twist.

Ramos Gin Fizz

Serve in a Collins or highball glass.

4 oz. gin	2 tsp. sugar syrup
1 oz. lime juice	2 tsp. heavy cream
1 oz. lemon juice	1 egg white *
Several dashes orange flower water	Club soda to fill

In a shaker or blender with cracked ice combine all ingredients except for the club soda. Shake or blend vigorously. Pour into the serving glasses. Add club soda to fill. Recipe makes two drinks. (Orange flower water is an extract of orange blossom and is available at gourmet stores.)

* Raw egg may be a source of salmonella bacteria. You may wish to avoid drinks calling for raw egg yolk or white.

Gin Cobbler

Serve in an old-fashioned or lowball glass.

2 oz. gin	Club soda to fill
1 tsp. orgeat syrup	Orange slice

Stir the gin and orgeat in the serving glass with ice; cracked ice works best. Fill with club soda. Garnish with an orange slice.

Red Lion Cocktail

Serve in a chilled cocktail glass.

1 oz. gin	¹/₂ oz. orange juice
1 oz. Grand Marnier	¹/₂ oz. lemon juice

Combine all ingredients in a shaker or blender with cracked ice. Shake or blend vigorously. Strain into the serving glass.

The Vider Vorld of Vodka

Coffee Cooler

Serve in a large old-fashioned glass.

1¹/₂ oz. vodka   4 oz. iced coffee

1 oz. Kahlúa   Scoop of coffee ice cream

1 oz. heavy cream

Combine all ingredients except the ice cream in a shaker. Shake vigorously and pour into the serving glass. Top with the ice cream.

Cosmopolitan

Serve in a cocktail glass.

³/₄ oz. vodka   1 oz. cranberry juice

¹/₂ oz. triple sec   ¹/₂ oz. lime juice

Shake with ice; serve up in a cocktail glass. Garnish with a lemon twist.

Dubonnet Fizz

Serve on the rocks in a highball glass.

1 oz. vodka   Club soda to fill

3 oz. Dubonnet rouge   Lemon peel

Combine the vodka and Dubonnet in the serving glass one-third full of ice. Add the club soda to fill and garnish with the lemon twist.

Russian Cocktail
Serve in a chilled cocktail glass.

1 oz. vodka   1 oz. white crème de cacao

1 oz. gin

Combine the ingredients with cracked ice in a shaker. Shake vigorously, then strain into the serving glass.

More Produce from Kentucky and Tennessee

Bourbon Cooler
Serve in a chilled Collins glass.

3 oz. bourbon	Club soda to fill
1/2 oz. grenadine	Pineapple stick
1 tsp. sugar syrup	Orange slice
Few dashes peppermint schnapps	Maraschino cherry
Few dashes orange bitters (optional)	

Combine all ingredients except the fruit and club soda in a shaker with cracked ice. Shake vigorously, then pour into the serving glass. Fill with club soda. Garnish with the fruit.

Champagne Julep
Serve in a Collins glass.

6 mint leaves	3 oz. bourbon
Mint sprig	Brut champagne
1 tsp. sugar syrup	

In the bottom of the serving glass, *muddle* (stir and mash) six mint leaves in the sugar syrup. Fill glass two-thirds with cracked ice. Add bourbon. Stir vigorously. Add champagne to fill. Garnish with a mint sprig.

Commodore Cocktail
Serve in a chilled cocktail glass.

1$^1/_2$ oz. bourbon

$^3/_4$ oz. white crème de cacao

$^1/_2$ oz. lemon juice

Combine all ingredients in a shaker with cracked ice. Shake vigorously and strain into the serving glass.

Whiskey Cobbler
Serve in a goblet or large snifter.

1 tsp. sugar syrup	Dash curaçao
1 tsp. orgeat syrup or amaretto liquor	Mint sprig
2 oz. blended whiskey	

Fill the goblet or snifter with crushed ice. Add the sugar and orgeat (or amaretto). Stir well. Add whiskey. Stir again, so that frost forms on the outside of the serving glass. Dash on curaçao and garnish with the mint sprig.

'Round the Blend—Again

Frisco Sour
Serve in a sour glass.

1$^1/_2$ oz. blended whiskey	1 tsp. lime juice
$^3/_4$ oz. Benedictine	Dash grenadine
1 tsp. lemon juice	Orange slice

Combine all ingredients except orange slice in a shaker with ice. Shake vigorously, then strain into the serving glass. Garnish with the orange slice.

Horse's Neck
Serve in a Collins glass.

1 lemon

3 oz. blended whiskey

Ginger ale to fill

Peel the lemon in one continuous strip and place it in the serving glass. Fill the glass one-third with ice cubes. Add whiskey. Squeeze a few drops of lemon juice over the whiskey, then add ginger ale to fill.

Scotland and Ireland Revisited

Affinity Cocktail
Serve in a chilled cocktail glass.

1 oz. scotch	Liberal dashes Angostura bitters
1 oz. dry sherry	Lemon twist
1 oz. port	Maraschino cherry

Combine all ingredients except fruit in a mixing glass with ice. Stir well, then strain into the serving glass and garnish with the twist and cherry.

Flying Scot
Serve in a chilled old-fashioned glass.

1 1/2 oz. scotch

1 oz. sweet vermouth

Few dashes sugar syrup

Few dashes Angostura bitters

Combine all ingredients in a shaker with cracked ice. Pour into the serving glass.

Kinsale Cooler
Serve in a chilled Collins glass.

$1^1/_2$ oz. Irish whiskey

1 oz. Irish Mist

1 oz. lemon juice

Equal portions club soda and ginger ale to fill

Lemon twist

Combine all ingredients except the sodas and the twist in a shaker with cracked ice. Shake vigorously, then pour into the serving glass and add equal portions of club soda and ginger ale to fill. Garnish with the twist.

Royal Rob Roy
Serve in a chilled cocktail glass.

$1^1/_2$ oz. scotch

$1^1/_2$ oz. Drambuie

$1/_4$ oz. dry vermouth

$1/_4$ oz. sweet vermouth

Maraschino cherry

Combine all ingredients except the cherry in a shaker with cracked ice. Shake vigorously, then strain into the serving glass and garnish with the cherry.

Rum Round Two

Cocoa-Colada
Serve in a chilled Collins glass.

$1^1/_2$ oz. Myers's rum

1 oz. Kahlúa

2 oz. pineapple juice

1 oz. cream of coconut

Orange slice

Combine all ingredients except the orange slice in a blender with a scoop of crushed ice. Blend until smooth, then pour into the serving glass and garnish with the orange slice.

Frozen Daiquiri

*Serve in a chilled cocktail glass or in an
American-style (saucer) champagne glass.*

2 oz. light rum

$^1/_2$ oz. lime juice

1 tsp. sugar

Combine all ingredients in a blender with at least
4 oz. of crushed ice. Blend at low speed until snowy,
then pour into the serving glass.

Frozen Peach Daiquiri

*Serve in a chilled cocktail glass or in an
American-style (saucer) champagne glass.*

$1^1/_2$ oz. light rum

$^1/_2$ oz. lime juice

1 tbsp. diced peaches (fresh, canned, or frozen)

1 tsp. lemon juice

Combine all ingredients in a blender with at least
4 oz. of crushed ice. Blend at low speed until snowy,
then pour into the serving glass.

Nutty Colada

Serve in a chilled Collins glass.

2 oz. amaretto

1 oz. gold rum

$1^1/_2$ oz. cream of coconut

2 oz. pineapple juice

Pineapple slice

Combine all ingredients except the pineapple slice
in a blender with a scoop of crushed ice. Blend
until smooth, then pour into the serving glass
and garnish with the pineapple slice.

Pineapple Daiquiri
Serve in a chilled cocktail glass or wine glass.

2 oz. light rum   3 oz. pineapple juice

$1/2$ oz. Cointreau $1/4$ oz. lime juice

Combine all ingredients in a blender with at least 3 oz. of cracked ice. Blend with ice on frappé. Pour into the serving glass.

Rum Collins
Serve in a chilled Collins glass.

2 oz. light rum $1/2$ lime

1 oz. sugar syrup   Club soda to fill

Combine the rum and sugar syrup in the serving glass. Stir. Squeeze in lime juice, then drop in peel as garnish. Add a few ice cubes and club soda to fill.

Rum Old-Fashioned
Serve in a chilled old-fashioned glass.

1 tsp. sugar syrup   3 oz. gold rum

Splash water   Lime twist

Liberal dashes Angostura bitters   Orange twist

Combine sugar syrup and water in the serving glass. Stir. Add bitters and rum. Stir, then add several ice cubes. Garnish with the twists.

Rum Screwdriver

Serve in a chilled Collins glass.

2 oz. light rum

5 oz. orange juice

Orange slice

Combine rum and juice in a blender with cracked ice. Blend until smooth, then pour into the serving glass. Garnish with orange slice.

Rum Sour

Serve in a chilled sour glass.

2 oz. light or dark rum	1 tsp. orange juice
Juice of 1/2 lime	Orange slice
1 tsp. sugar syrup	Maraschino cherry

Combine all ingredients except fruit in a shaker with ice. Shake vigorously, then strain into the serving glass and garnish with the orange slice and cherry.

Scorpion

Serve in a chilled wine goblet.

2 oz. light rum	1 1/2 oz. lemon juice
1 oz. brandy	1/2 oz. orgeat syrup
2 oz. orange juice	Gardenia (if available)

Combine all ingredients except the gardenia in a blender with 3 oz. of shaved ice. Blend until smooth, then pour into the serving glass. Garnish with the gardenia.

Strawberry Colada
Serve in a chilled pilsner glass.

3 oz. gold rum

4 oz. commercial Pina Colada mix

1 oz. strawberries (fresh or frozen)

1 oz. strawberry liqueur or strawberry schnapps

Whole strawberry

Combine all ingredients except liqueur or schnapps and whole strawberry in a blender with cracked ice. Blend until smooth, then pour into the serving glass, top with the liqueur or schnapps, and garnish with the whole strawberry.

Return to the Halls of Montezuma

Golden Margarita
Serve in a chilled lowball glass rimmed with salt.

2 oz. gold tequila	Coarse salt
1 oz. curaçao	Lime slice
3/4 oz. lime juice	

Combine all ingredients except salt and lime slice in a shaker with cracked ice. Shake vigorously, then pour into the serving glass. Garnish with the lime slice.

Tequila Collins
Serve on the rocks in a tall Collins glass.

1 1/2 oz. white tequila	Club soda to fill
1 oz. lemon juice	Maraschino cherry
Sugar syrup to taste	

Pour tequila, lemon juice, and sugar syrup over ice in the serving glass. Stir, then add club soda to fill. Garnish with the cherry.

Tequila Gimlet

Serve on the rocks in an old-fashioned glass.

1^1/$_2$ oz. white or gold tequila

1 oz. Rose's lime juice

Lime wedge

Combine the tequila and lime juice over ice in the serving glass. Stir, then garnish with the lime wedge.

Tequila Manhattan

1^1/$_2$ oz. gold tequila

Dash or two sweet vermouth

Lime slice

Combine tequila and vermouth in a shaker with ice. Shake vigorously, then strain into the serving glass. Garnish with the lime slice.

Tequila Maria

Serve in a chilled large (double) old-fashioned glass.

1^1/$_2$ oz. white or gold tequila

4 oz. tomato juice

Juice of ^{1}/$_4$ lime

^{1}/$_2$ tsp. fresh grated horseradish

Liberal dashes Worcestershire sauce

Liberal dashes Tabasco sauce

Pinch white pepper

Pinch celery salt

Pinch oregano

Combine all ingredients in a mixing glass half filled with cracked ice. Stir, then pour into the serving glass.

Tequila Sour

Serve in a chilled cocktail glass.

1¹/₂ oz. tequila

1 oz. lime or lemon juice

1 tsp. confectioner's sugar

Combine all ingredients in a shaker with ice. Shake vigorously, then strain into the serving glass.

Tequila Stinger

Serve in a chilled cocktail glass.

1¹/₂ oz. gold tequila

³/₄ oz. white crème de menthe

Combine ingredients in a shaker with cracked ice. Shake vigorously, then pour into the serving glass.

Another Snifter

Between the Sheets

Serve in a chilled cocktail glass.

1¹/₂ oz. cognac

1 oz. light rum

³/₄ oz. curaçao (may substitute triple sec)

¹/₂ oz. lemon juice

Combine all ingredients in a shaker with ice. Shake vigorously, then strain into the serving glass.

Bombay

Serve in a chilled old-fashioned glass.

1 oz. brandy	1/2 tsp. curaçao
1 oz. dry vermouth	Dash Pernod
1/2 oz. sweet vermouth	Orange slice

Combine all ingredients except orange slice in a shaker with cracked ice. Shake vigorously, then pour into the serving glass. Garnish with the orange slice.

Brandy Fizz

Serve in a chilled highball glass.

3 oz. brandy	1/2 oz. sugar syrup
1 1/2 oz. lemon juice	Club soda to fill

Combine all ingredients except soda in a shaker with cracked ice. Shake vigorously, then pour into the serving glass. Add club soda to fill. Additional ice cubes are optional. Omit the club soda, and you have a Brandy Fix.

Brandy Julep

Serve in a chilled large (double) old-fashioned glass.

6 mint leaves	Brandy to fill
1 tsp. honey	Mint sprig
Splash water	Powdered sugar

Combine the mint leaves, honey, and a splash of water in the serving glass. Muddle (mash and stir) until the leaves are well bruised. Fill serving glass with shaved ice. Add brandy to fill. Stir well so that glass frosts. Add additional brandy and ice as necessary to fill. *Glass should be full and thoroughly frosted.* Garnish with sprigs, then dust with powdered sugar.

Brandy Manhattan

Serve in a chilled cocktail glass.

2 oz. brandy

Dash Angostura bitters

$^1/_2$ oz. sweet or dry vermouth

Maraschino cherry

Combine all ingredients except cherry in a mixing glass one-third full of ice. Stir well, then strain into the serving glass. Garnish with the cherry.

Brandy Old-Fashioned

Serve in a chilled old-fashioned glass.

1 sugar cube

Liberal dashes Angostura bitters

Splash water

3 oz. brandy

Lemon twist

Put sugar cube in the serving glass, dash on bitters, and add a splash of water. Muddle (mash and stir) until the sugar cube is dissolved. Half fill glass with ice cubes and add brandy. Garnish with twist.

Index

A

Abbey Cocktail, 31-33
Affinity Cocktail, 182
aging brandy, 136
Alabama Slammer Highball and Shooter, 148
Alexander's Sister de Menthe, 138
Alexander's Sister Kahlúa, 138
Alternative Whiskey Sour, 84
Amaretto Café, 152
apéritif wines, 5
Apple Blossom with Juice, 139
Apricot Brandy Fizz and Sour, 140
apéritif, 165
arrack, 165

B

B & B, 142
B & B Collins, 143
B-52, 174
Bahama Mama, 174
Bairn, 103
Bal Harbour, 94
Ballylickey Belt, 107
Banana Daiquiri, 117
bar mix, see sour mix
barback, 166
Barbados rum, 113
Barracuda, 145
bars
    glassware, 10-13
    stocked items, 1-8
    tools, 8
Bermuda Cocktail, 37
Berta's Special, 132
Between the Sheets, 120, 189
Big Apple, 162
bitters, 6
Black Hawk, 85
Black Russian, 45
Black Stripe, 118
blended scotches, 100
blended whiskey, 78
Blended Whiskey Old Fashioned, 83
Blood and Sand, 105
Bloody Blossom, 41
Bloody Mary, 40
Blue Hawaiian, 119
Blue Margarita, 129
Bluegrass Cocktail, 67
Bobby Burns, 105
Bombay, 190
bourbon, 63
Bourbon Cobbler, 68

Bourbon Collins
  Augmented, 69
  Unadorned, 68
Bourbon Cooler, 180
Bourbon Manhattan, 69
Bourbon Old Fashioned, 70
Bourbon Rose (dark), 70
Bourbon Rose (pale), 70
Bourbon Sidecar, 71
Bourbon Sour, 71
Bow Street Special, 108
Brain, 174
branch water, 166
brandy
  aging process, 136
  flavored, 137
  snifters, 13
    chilling, 92
  standard stock in home
    bars, 5
  V.O. (very old) label, 136
  V.S.O.P. (very superior old
    pale) label, 136
Brandy Alexander, 137
Brandy and Soda, 138
Brandy Fizz, 190
Brandy Flip, 139
Brandy Julep, 190
Brandy Manhattan, 191
Brandy Old-Fashioned, 191
Brave Bull, 132
Brigadoon, 106
Bronx Cocktail, 32
Burning Blue Mountain, 161

C

Café Bonaparte, 153
Café Foster, 123
Café Kahlúa, 146
Café Marnier, 153
Café Mexicano, 153
Café Zurich, 155

Calypso, 122
Campari, 28
Canadian Old Fashioned, 83
Canadian whisky, 78, 87-88
Cape Codder, 41
carbonated mixers, 2
celery stalks, 7
champagne, 21
  Champagne Cooler, 143
  Champagne Julep, 180
  flutes and glasses, 12
Changuirongo, 131
Cherry Blossom, 141
Cherry Cola Rum, 114
Cherry Hill, 141
Chicago, 144
chilling
  brandy snifters, 92
  glasses, 23, 58
chocolate martini, 59
Christmas Rum Punch, 162
ciders, hard versus
  sweet, 159
Cinzano, 27
citrus drinks, 41-44, 49,
  67-70, 82
cocktails, 8
  glasses, 11
  shaken versus stirred, 17
Coco Loco, 133
Cocoa-Colada, 183
Coffee Blazer, 163
Coffee Cooler, 179
coffee drinks, 45, 152-155
cognac, alembics, 136
Collins glasses, 10
comfort drinks, 157
Comfort Mocha, 155
Commodore Cocktail, 181
congeners, 167
copita glasses, 11
cordial glasses, 12
cordials, see liqueurs
corkscrew, screw-pull, 21

Cornell Cocktail, 36
Cosmopolitan, 179
Crazy Nun, 132
Creamy Irish Coffee, 154
Cuba Libre, 114

D

daiquiris, 21, 116
Demerara rum, 113
Dog Sled, 87
Drambuie, 103
drink mixes, standard stock
    in home bars, 3
dry gin, 26
Dry Mahoney, 72
Dry Manhattan, 80
dry martinis, 52-54
Dry Rye Manhattan, 96
dry vermouth, 52
dry vodka martinis, 55
Dubonnet Cocktail, 177
Dubonnet Fizz, 179
Dundee Dream, 104

E-F

Elk's Own, 97
exotic liqueurs, 5

fizzes, 92
fizz glasses, 14
flambé, 161, 168
flaming drinks, 159
    Big Apple, 162
    Burning Blue
        Mountain, 161
    Christmas Rum Punch,
        162
    Coffee Blazer, 163
    warnings, 160

flavored brandy, 137
flips, 92
flutes, 12
Flying Grasshopper, 47
Flying Scot, 182
fortified coffee, 152
fortified wine, 168
fraise, 137
framboise, 137
freezes, 21
Frisco Cocktail, 94
Frisco Sour, 181
Frontenac Cocktail, 87
frosting glassware, 24
frozen drinks, 21
    daiquiris, 184
    Frozen Julep, 66
    margaritas, 128-129
Fuzzy Navel, 43

G

garbage, 7
garnishes, 6-7
Gimlet with Fresh Lime, 29
gin
    mixability, 26
    with liqueur recipes, 36
gin and bitters, 27
Gin and Campari, 27
Gin and Ginger, 28
Gin and Grapefruit Juice, 38
Gin and It martini, 61
Gin and Sin, 27
Gin and Soda, 28
Gin and Tonic, 29
Gin Cobbler, 178
Gin Daisy, 35
Gin Fizz, 34
gin Gibson, 56
gin martini, 52
Gin Rickey, 35

Gin Screwdriver, 30-31
Gin Sidecar, 35
Gin Sling, 36
Gin Sour, 33
glasses
    brandy snifter, 13
    chilling, 23, 58
    cocktail glass, 11
    Collins glass, 10
    frosting, 24
    highball glass, 10
    lowball glass, 10
    old-fashioned glass, 10
    rim-flavoring, 24
    salting, 24
    sherry glass, 11
    shot glass, 12
    sour glass, 11
    specialty glasses, 13
gold tequila, 126
Golden Margarita, 187
Grafton Street Sour, 109
grain scotch, 100
Grand Hotel, 146
Grapefruit Cooler, 82
Grasshopper, 149
Grenadine, 4

H

hard cider, 159
Harvey Wallbanger, 43
Hawaiian Martini, 59
highball glass, 10
highballs, 16
Highland Fling with
  Milk, 102
Highland Fling with Sweet
  Vermouth, 102
home bars
    brandies, 5
    carbonated mixers, 2

    drink mixes, 3
    garnishes, 6-7
    liqueurs, 2
    liquor, 1
    swizzle sticks, 8
Horse's Neck, 182
Hot Buttered Rum, 156
hot drinks, 152-155, 158,
  162-163
Hot Grog, 155
Hot Toddy, 156
Hot Toddy with
  Bourbon, 157

I

Indian River Rye
  Cocktail, 97
Irish Mist liqueur
  drinks, 107
Irish whiskey, 106-108, 154
Italian Coffee, 152

J

Jamaican Coffee, 122, 154
Jamaican rum, 113
Jell-O Shots, 175
jiggers, measuring, 8, 16
John Collins, 68
juices, stocking bar, 3

K

Kamikaze, 44, 175
King's Peg, 144
Kinsale Cooler, 183
kirsch, 137

L

Ladies' Cocktail, 86
lemon twists, 6
light whiskey, 78
lime wedges, 7
liqueurs
    exotic, 5
    standard stock in home
        bars, 2
liquor
    speed dispensing, 23
    standard stock in home
        bars, 1
London dry gin, 26
Lone Tree, 32
Long Island Iced Tea, 175
Lord Baltimore's Cup, 94
lowball glass, 10

M

macerate, 169
Madiera Cocktail, 87
malt, 100
malt scotch, 100
Manhattan, 69, 80
maraschino cherries, 7
marc brandy, 137
margaritas, 21
martini glasses, 14
Martini Romana, 60
martinis
    chocolate martini, 59
    degree of dryness, 54
    Gin and It, 61
    gin Gibson, 56
    Hawaiian Martini, 59
    Martini Romana, 60
    Rum Martini, 60
    stirred, 18

    Sweet Martini, 61
    Tequini, 60
master blender, 79, 170
Matador, 131
Mazatlan, 147
measuring jiggers, 16
Melon Ball, 49, 147
Melon Ball Sunrise, 176
Melon Patch, 147
Midori Sour, 176
Millionaire Cocktail, 72
Mint Juleps, 65-66
mirabelle, 137
mixed grain whiskey,
    78, 170
molasses as basis of
    rum, 112
muddling, 66
Mulled Cider, 158
Mulled Claret, 158

N

Navy Grog, 118
neat whiskey, 64
Negroni, 28
New Yorker, 84
Nutty Colada, 184

O

Old Fashioned, 70
Old Fashioned
    Manhattan, 80
old-fashioned glass, 10
olives, 7
Orange Blossom, 31
Original Sazerac, 74

P

Paddy Cocktail, 109
Pale Bourbon Rose, 70
Pancho Villa Shooter, 126
parfait glasses, 14
Peach Daiquiri, 117
Peach Fizz, 142
Peachtree Sling, 142
pear brandy, 137
pearl onions, gin or vodka
    Gibsons, 7, 57
Perfect Manhattan, 81
Perfect Martini, 56
Perfect Rye Manhattan, 96
piña coladas, 21, 115
Pineapple Daiquiri, 185
Pink Gin, 27
Pink Lady, 38
Pink Rye, 95
Pink Squirrel, 149
Plantation Punch, 122
Planter's Punch, 121
pony glasses, 12-13
pouring style for
    bartenders, 22
pousse-café glasses, 13
Presbyterian, 73
proprietary liqueurs, 171
Puerto Rican rum, 113

R

Ramos Gin Fizz, 178
really dry martinis, 56
recipes
    brandy drinks
    coffee drinks, 45, 123, 146,
        153-155
    citrus drinks, 41-44, 49,
        67-70, 82
    fizz drinks, 82
    frozen margaritas, 128-129

gin drinks, 177-178
rum drinks, 183-187
scotch drinks, 182-183
shaken cocktails, 19
stirred cocktails, 18
tequila drinks, 130-131,
    187-189
unusual drinks, 174-177
vodka drinks, 179-180
whiskey drinks, 181-182
Red Lion Cocktail, 178
rickey, 34, 171
rim-flavoring, glassware, 24
Rock and Rye Cooler, 91
Rock and Rye Toddy, 91
Roman Coffee, 152
Rose's lime juice, 4
Royal Rob Roy, 183
rum
    Bahama Mama, 174
    Barbados rum, 113
    Burning Blue
        Mountain, 161
    Christmas Rum
        Punch, 162
    Cocoa-Colada, 183
    Columbian rum, 113
    distillation methods, 112
    fermentation process, 112
    Frozen Daiquiri, 184
    Frozen Peach Daiquiri, 184
    Hot Buttered Rum, 156
    Hot Grog, 155
    Jamaican rum, 113
    Nutty Colada, 184
    Pineapple Daiquiri, 185
    Puerto Rican rum, 113
    Rum Collins, 185
    Rum martini, 60
    Rum Old-Fashioned, 185
    Rum Screwdriver, 186
    Rum Sour, 186
    Scorpion, 186
    taste, 112

Rum Collins, 185
Rum Old-Fashioned, 185
Rum Screwdriver, 186
Rum Sour, 186
Russian Cocktail, 180
Russian Coffee, 45
Rusty Nail, 102
rye
    Bal Harbour, 94
    decreasing popularity, 89
    drinking guidelines, 90
    Dry Rye Manhattan, 96
    Elk's Own, 97
    fizzes, 92
    flips, 92
    Frisco Cocktail, 94
    grain lineage, 89
    Indian River Rye
      Cocktail, 97
    Lord Baltimore's Cup, 94
    Perfect Rye Manhattan, 96
    Pink Rye, 95
    Rye Manhattan, 95
Rye Fizz, 92
Rye Flip, 92
Rye Manhattan, 95

S

salting glassware, 24
Sangrita, 127
Saskatoon Stinger, 88
Scorpion, 186
scotch, 101-102
    Affinity Cocktail, 182
    Bairn, 103
    Flying Scot, 182
    glassware, 101
    ice purity, 101
    Kinsale Cooler, 183
    Royal Rob Roy, 183

Rusty Nail, 102
    with liqueurs, 103
Scotch Orange Fix, 104
Scotch Sangaree, 104
Scotch Smash, 105
Screwdriver, 42
Seven and 7, 86
Sex on the Beach, 43-44
shaken cocktails, 17-19
sherry glasses, 11
shooters, 44
shot glasses, 12
Sidecar, 139
Simple Sazerac, 73
simple syrup, 4
Singapore Sling, 38
single malt scotches, 100
slings, 36-37
sloe gin, 171
Sloe Gin Fizz, 148
sour glasses, 11
sour mix, 3-4
Spanish vodka martini, 59
specialty glasses, 13
specific gravity, 171
speedpourers, 8, 22-23
spritzer, 172
Stinger, 139
stirred cocktails
    versus shaken cocktails, 17
    vodka gimlets, 18
stocking home bars, 1-8
straight vodka, 40
straight whiskey, 78
Strawberry Colada, 187
Strawberry Daiquiri, 117
sugar syrup, 4
surface tension, 172
sweet cider, 159
Sweet Martini, 61
Swiss army knife, 8
swizzle sticks, 8

T

Tennessee whiskey, 67
tequila, 125-126
tequila añejo, 126
Tequila Collins, 187
Tequila Gimlet, 188
Tequila Manhattan, 134, 188
Tequila Maria, 188
Tequila Sour, 189
Tequila Stinger, 189
Tequila Sunrise, 130
Tequila Sunset, 131
Tequini, 60
The Darb, 36
three count technique for
    speed pourer, 16
Toasted Almond, 177
toddy, 91, 156
Tom Collins, 30
Top Shelf Margarita, 130
traditional shot of
    tequila, 126
twin lever corkscrews, 21

U-V

unusual drinks, 174-177

V.O. (very old) brandy, 136
V.S.O.P. (very superior old
    pale) brandy, 136
Venezuelan rum, 113
vodka
    gimlets, 18
    martinis, 52, 55, 59
    straight, 40
    with citrus juices, 41
    with coffee liqueur, 45
Vodka Collins, 46
Vodka Cooler, 47
Vodka Gibson, 57
Vodka Gimlet, 42
Vodka Grasshopper, 47
Vodka Sour, 48
Vodka Stinger, 48
Vodka Tonic, 48

W-Z

Ward Eight, 75
whiskey, 63-64, 79
    blended whiskey, 78
    Canadian whisky, 78
    light, 78
    neat, 64
    role of master blender, 78
    rye, 89-90
    straight, 78
    Tennessee whiskey, 67
Whiskey Cobbler, 181
Whiskey Curaçao Fizz, 82
Whiskey Daisy, 85
Whiskey Fizz, 82
Whiskey Rickey, 83
Whiskey Sour, 19, 84
White Russian, 45
white tequila, 126
wines, opening, 21
Woo Woo, 177
wort, 172

Zombie, 119